COUNTRY LIVING
happy halloween!

BEWITCHING PARTIES AND RECIPES, ENCHANTING PUMPKINS
AND DECORATIONS, PLUS LOTS OF OTHER SPINE-TINGLING IDEAS

HEARST BOOKS

A division of Sterling Publishing Co., Inc.

New York / London
www.sterlingpublishing.com

Designer: Anna Christian
Project Editor: Sarah Scheffel

Library of Congress Cataloging-in-Publication Data is available.

10 9 8 7 6 5 4 3 2 1

Published by Hearst Books
A division of Sterling Publishing Co., Inc.
387 Park Avenue South, New York, NY 10016

Country Living and Hearst Books are trademarks of Hearst Communications, Inc.
www.countryliving.com

For information about custom editions, special sales, premium and corporate
purchases, please contact Sterling Special Sales Department at 800-805-5489 or
specialsales@sterlingpublishing.com.

Distributed in Canada by Sterling Publishing
c/o Canadian Manda Group, 165 Dufferin Street
Toronto, Ontario, Canada M6K 3H6

Distributed in Australia by Capricorn Link (Australia) Pty. Ltd.
P.O. Box 704, Windsor, NSW 2756 Australia

Manufactured in China

Sterling ISBN 978-1-58816-784-2

contents

introduction

As Halloween approaches, anticipation is in the air. Luckily, there are lots of fun activities to keep you busy while you look forward to the most playful night of the year.

There's the all-important trip to the farmers' market or pumpkin patch to select the perfect pumpkin for this year's jack-o'-lantern. Then there is costume planning, possibly for a whole family of little goblins, robots, and fairies. Decorating the house, indoors and out, is always a pleasure, as is planning a party, if you choose to entertain more than the bands of merry trick-or-treaters who show up on your doorstep!

To help you celebrate this high-spirited holiday, the editors of *Country Living* have compiled all of the best tricks and treats in a single book. Want to transform your pride and joy into a ferocious lion? We provide step-by-step instructions and loads of inspiration for adorable costumes your kids will love. Looking for cool pumpkin-carving ideas? We share an entire pumpkin patch worth of spooky jack-o'-lanterns and artful pumpkins, all gloriously photographed in full color.

If you're planning an All Hallows' Eve party, and seasonal recipes and treats to go with it, look no further. We include party plans and menus for three different crowds: a rollicking kids' bash, a thoroughly grown-up fête, and a pumpkin-carving party for the whole gang. Intermixed are recipes for dozens of devilishly delicious holiday snacks and treats that everyone will love.

Whatever you're looking for, you'll find all your Halloween inspiration right here. So, go ahead, gather together your family and friends (along with a heap of glitter, candy corns, and carving tools), and get ready for the happiest Halloween ever!

spooky jack-o'-lanterns & artful pumpkins

get out your carving kit!

What would Halloween be without pumpkins? Large or small, smooth or gnarled, pumpkins and their jack-o'-lantern "offspring" are an essential hallmark of the holiday. We all look forward to choosing and carving our annual pumpkin (or pumpkins). Seeing how our neighbors carve their jack-o'-lanterns is almost as much fun.

Legend holds that the Irish get credit for the jack-o'-lantern. Though renditions of the tale vary, it seems our grinning Jack evolved from lanterns carved out of turnips and carried in Celtic celebrations of the Day of the Dead. In recent years, pumpkin carving has evolved from crudely cut faces to sophisticated, intricate designs that are just as likely to become the centerpieces for an autumn dinner party as they are to liven up a round of trick-or-treating.

This chapter is all about making the most of that pumpkin—and all of its squash and gourd cousins—in your seasonal decorating. Included are many inventive, out-of-the-ordinary jack-o'-lanterns. But here, too, are sophisticated and unusual ideas for using the farmstand's bounty to imbue your home with beauty all season long. Many pumpkins are illuminated from within, and many are etched only on the surface; some are so easy you'll want to launch an assembly line, while others take a bit more patience to complete.

Whether you choose to create a spooky pumpkin creature or a stylish gourd lantern, do read these basics before digging in. We hope you'll be inspired to decorate, entertain, and celebrate with wonderful new twists on pumpkin carving and to create your own style of pumpkin chic.

CHOOSING WHAT TO CARVE

Pumpkins, the most traditional choice, range in size from the orange Jack Be Little and the white Baby Boo (each of which grows to no more than about 3 inches wide and 2 inches tall) to the mammoth prize-winning Atlantic Giant, which can weigh in at over a whopping 1,000 pounds.

But that's just the beginning. Kuri, Kabocha, Hokkaido, Cushaw, Lakota, Delicata—what sounds like a magical incantation is just a partial list of the many varieties of squash that are readily available today, joining the likes of acorn and butternut and the whimsical-sounding sweet dumpling. (All pumpkins and gourds are, technically, squashes.)

Hard-skinned winter squashes, such as acorn and butternut, and gourds require a bit more patience to carve, especially if the surface is prominently ridged or warty, but they can yield bewitching creations. Consider some of the stranger-looking species, too— for instance, the gooseneck gourd or the bumpy, pale blue-green-skinned Hubbard squash. Species with contrasting colors of skin and flesh, such as the white Lumina, with its orange interior, will unleash the artist in you.

Choose a specimen that has no soft spots or signs of mold or rot. Even if you intend to remove the stem, it's best to purchase a pumpkin with one, as the flesh is subject to quicker decay once the stem is broken. (Never use the stem as a handle.) You don't necessarily need a "perfect" shape; surface bumps and quirky contours can all become part of your design. Don't worry about caked-on dirt, either. Much of this can be removed with a stiff-bristled brush, a damp sponge or rag, or a quick rinse.

Illuminating Ideas

When lit from within, a jack-o'-lantern's persona emerges. Even the simplest **designs look magical glowing in the dark**, and any little "mistakes" will no longer matter.

{ CANDLE POWER }

Use candles safely. Place them only in steady pumpkins that won't be bumped or pose a hazard to children. A **votive candle** in a glass holder—or more than one, for brightness—or a **taper candle** that's been burned long enough to become a bit stubby are the most reliable choices. To anchor a taper, scoop out a hole, drip a little melted wax into it, and immediately stick the candle in to secure it. Another trick is to cut a hole in the bottom of the pumpkin and slide the pumpkin over a candle. Light candles with a fireplace match or a long electric lighter.

{ ELECTRIC POWER }

A small flashlight or **battery-operated pumpkin light** (available with a steady or blinking beam) is a safe flame-free alternative to candles; for a brighter glow, use more than one. You may wish to set the light on a square of folded plastic wrap to prevent it from becoming slimy.

Plug-in electric options include 25- to 40-watt bulbs in outdoor utility light sockets (great for thick pumpkins that need stronger illumination) and strands of **outdoor Christmas lights** (with these, you can create a pathway of luminaria). Choose red or green lights instead of white for extra eeriness. The new indoor-outdoor LED (light-emitting-diode) strings of lights work well, too. To keep lights clean, cut the pumpkin's opening in the bottom and carve a narrow channel in the back of the base to allow the wire to escape without being pinched.

For lighting a pumpkin-filled porch, you can keep it classic with lanterns or hang **strings of carnival lights**. For a jollier touch, invest in strings of lights with bulb covers shaped like pumpkins or ghosts.

Ask a panel of experienced pumpkin carvers about their favorite tools and each person will tell you something different. Long, slender kitchen knives are preferred by some because they cut a clean, smooth line; others vouch for a stubby knife with a serrated edge (easier to control, they say).

Around Halloween time, stores with holiday supplies carry pumpkin-carving kits that contain tools designed for children to use easily and safely. Art supply stores carry sculpting tools that make it easy to carve with great detail.

Store your pumpkin in a cool, dark place and do not carve until a day or two before Halloween; once carved, most pumpkins only last a few days. When you're ready, gather the tools you need:

❋ **Lots of newspaper** is necessary to protect your work space.

❋ **A melon scooper and serving-size spoons** are great for scooping out and scraping the insides of pumpkins.

❋ **A pencil or dry-erase marker** makes it easy to sketch designs on the pumpkin.

❋ **An 8-inch carving knife** with a narrow blade will do the carving.

❋ **A small paring knife** with a narrow blade works best for corners and curves, and also is good for neatening rough edges. Use the handle end to tap out circles and other shapes once cut.

❋ **Different sizes of candles** may be needed to fit inside the pumpkins, though the 3-inch-high ones found in supermarkets usually do the job. Standard matches or a lighter are adequate for small pumpkins or larger ones with a door carved into the back. To light a big jack-o'-lantern that opens at the top, long fireplace matches are handy.

❋ **Small saucers or votive glasses** can be used to hold candles in place. Drip a few drops of hot wax on a small saucer that will fit easily through the opening in the pumpkin. Hold the candle in place on the plate while the wax hardens.

OPTIONAL TOOLS—FOR ADULT USE ONLY

If you want to go beyond the simple triangles and squares of standard jack-o'-lanterns, some additional tools are required:

❋ **A stainless-steel round hole cutter,** available in art supply stores, is good for cutting perfect circles in jack-o'-lanterns. An apple corer works well, too.

❋ **A loop,** a clay tool available in art supply stores, is perfect for making spirals, flames (see photo, opposite), and other designs that don't go all the way through the pumpkin skin, creating a translucent effect.

❋ **Medium wood gouges**—sculpture carving tools available in art supply stores—can be used for layering and for circles. Place the tip of the gouge under the jack-o'-lantern's eyes and tap downward on the handle with a wooden mallet. This will cut away the top layer of pumpkin flesh to create a little teardrop for a sad look. Or insert the gouge into the pumpkin flesh, turn, and pull out to complete a circular shape.

❋ **A power drill with a hole-cutter drill bit** makes carving larger pumpkins with thick shells easier. Use them to control the cutting of exact designs, such as the Polka-Dot Pumpkins on page 52.

❋ **Use a linoleum cutter or chisel** for etching and inscribing surface designs, as shown in the Falling Autumn Leaves pumpkin, page 47.

PUMPKIN-CARVING TIPS

✳ Choose a large, plump pumpkin with a long, strong stem for the best jack-o'-lantern.

✳ Sketch out your ideas on paper before you draw and carve the pumpkin. Perhaps the natural shape of the pumpkin will inspire a design.

✳ Keep a decent distance between the eyes, nose, and mouth when carving, or else the pumpkin might collapse.

✳ Select candles that are the right height for the size of the pumpkin. Candles that are too tall will burn the top of the pumpkin.

✳ Save the pumpkin seeds for roasting; they make a crunchy, nutritious snack (see page 109).

PUMPKIN CARVING WITH CHILDREN

✳ Never let children carve pumpkins alone.

✳ Let children do as much work as possible, with the exception of using sharp tools.

✳ Make the features large so that they are easy to cut out. This also means more light will shine from the jack-o'-lantern.

✳ A child too young to use a knife can help draw the face and scoop out the seeds.

Eerie Props and Accessories

For sly or spectacular effects, your **jack-o'-lantern** can be embellished in many ways other than carving. To involve children who are too young to wield cutting tools, you can, of course, let them paint their own designs on pumpkins large and small (or let them mark designs for you to cut). But with some extra elements, you can really **dress up your gourd**.

{ THEATRICAL SPIRIT }

Think in terms of **wardrobe and props**. Find a pointy witch's hat or a straw garden hat from summers past to lend **sinister charm** or rustic flair to glowing faces. Let a toy arrow or an old scythe inspire the setting of a **grim and gruesome tableau**, set up for a frightful Halloween fête. Use artificial—and surprisingly convincing—crows, bats, rats, spiders, and spiderwebs (widely available in the weeks leading up to the holiday) to stage a spooky show. You'd be surprised: Even a single uncarved pumpkin with a faux blackbird perched on its stem has the power to **playfully startle a visitor** who catches a glimpse through the front window.

{ NATURAL WEIRDNESS }

Look in the garden, yard, and woods, at floral shops, garden centers, and the grocery store for natural add-ons. **Twigs are spindly arms** or eerie antennae. **Leaves or corn husks**, attached with floral u-pins, can look like a ruffled collar or, as shown in the Masked Goblin above left, a shaggy coiffure. Seedpods, which nature offers in such astonishing variety, are abundant this time of year; use them as eyes, horns, or even tongues. Try **sumac pods, pinecones, broom corn fronds, or cattails**—just carve a hole into which the materials will fit snugly. Even gourds themselves can be the add-ons. Don't be afraid to cut them apart to make eyes, ears, noses, or whatever else you can envision hiding in their round or coiled shapes.

CLASSIC JACK-O'-LANTERNS

In Celtic times, huge bonfires were set to frighten away the evil spirits believed to wander the land on All Hallow's Eve. Much later, Irish villagers paraded from house to house on this night, carrying lanterns made from turnips and beets. Once they immigrated here, the Irish found that the native American pumpkin was easier to carve and made a much bigger lantern. So the jack-o'-lantern was born.

1 Cover the work surface with newspapers. Cut off the tops of the pumpkins with the carving knife by making a 6-inch circular cut around the stems. Remove the tops and hollow out the pumpkins with a large spoon.

2 Sketch features on the pumpkin surfaces with a pencil. Cut out features with the carving knife and paring knife. To make a circle, insert the gouge into the pumpkin by tapping the gouge's handle with a hammer and twisting. Punch out the piece. For a 3-D effect, cut narrow, triangular holes in the nose areas and insert carrot pieces.

3 Without cutting through the pumpkins, use the loop to create wrinkles, hair, and other surface details by inserting the top of the loop and pulling just enough that the orange layer of skin comes off.

4 Melt the bottom of the candle and anchor it to the glass container. Insert the candles in the pumpkins and light with fireplace matches. Leave the tops off the pumpkins to prevent the candles from extinguishing.

PUMPKINS WITH PERSONALITY

MATERIALS

large pumpkins with stems intact (choose unusual shapes)

cranberries, nuts, and/or grapes

TOOLS

carving tools, such as a loop, half-round carving tool, and medium wood gouge (available in art supply stores)

drill fitted with a 1-inch hole-cutter drill bit

carving knife

By setting it on its side, with the stem serving as a nose, a pumpkin can go from round and plump to just plain comical. Around Halloween, there are so many pumpkins to choose from at farm stands and garden stores that finding a few with humorous potential should be easy and fun. Look for tall, skinny, or odd-shaped pumpkins with long, thick stems. The actual "carving" takes only a few minutes, as it is not necessary to clean out the insides. And since they are not hollowed out, they will stay fresher longer.

1 Cover the work surface with newspapers.

2 Turn each pumpkin to a side on which it will rest solidly. With the carving tools, create eyes, mouths, and teeth. Use the loop to create surface details, like teeth and whites of eyes. For circles, use the half-round carving tool or drill and drill bit. For slits, use the carving knife. Insert cranberries, nuts, or grapes in narrow slits to create eyes.

Sentry Style

An easy way to infuse the whole house with Halloween spirit is to carve many little jack-o'-lanterns, some with eyes only, and let them keep watch from tables, transoms, bookcases, nightstands, mantels, kitchen shelves, and other nooks and ledges. Leave some unlit—they're surprisingly devilish when they're dark within.

A BATTY WELCOME

MATERIALS

white acorn squashes

husks and kernels from Indian corn

toothpicks

screw-in hooks or drive hooks

brads or floral u-pins

twine or monofilament

TOOLS

large nail

awl

scissors

Hovering in the night air, these eerie flying mammals will guard the front door all through Halloween, yet each takes only minutes to make. Their white acorn-squash bodies and corn-husk wings will glow like ghosts in the darkness. Suspend them from a porch ceiling, the eaves of the house, or tree limbs—just be sure to keep their wings and fangs out of head-bumping range.

1 Work with the stem of the acorn squash as the top. With the large nail, gouge the squash's skin to make two holes for the corn-kernel eyes. Press the kernels into the holes so they are secure. With the awl, pierce two holes for the fangs; pierce the holes so that the fangs will point up or down or in different directions, as desired. Cut a toothpick in half and insert the blunt ends of the halves into the holes for fangs.

2 If there is no stem, screw or drive the hook into the stem end of the squash.

3 For the wings, use scissors to cut a scalloped edge on one side of each of two corn husks. Make sure you have a left and a right wing. Fasten each wing to the back of the squash with brads or floral u-pins.

4 Tie twine—or monofilament, for invisibility—to the stem or the hook for hanging.

SHIFTY-EYED CRITTERS

Every Hubbard squash, with its bluish-green skin and peculiar form, definitely has a menacing critter inside. Carve as many of these antennae-sprouting creatures as you like and let them keep watch, peering this way and that, to ward off spirits more ghastly than they. There are no airholes for flames, so use battery-operated lights inside.

MATERIALS

Hubbard squashes

long twigs

battery-operated lights or outdoor approved light sockets with 25- to 40-watt bulbs

TOOLS

carving knife

large spoon

pencil

paring knife

linoleum cutter or small chisel

drill fitted with a hole-cutter drill bit

1 Cut a door from the bottom of the rear of each squash and scrape out the seeds and the pulp. You will need to thin the walls behind where the eyes will be—the thinner the flesh, the brighter the glow.

2 Mark the half-moon outlines of the eyes with a pencil. Then mark smaller curves within the eyes for the pupils, making sure that each critter is looking in a different direction. With the paring knife, cut $\frac{1}{4}$ to $\frac{1}{2}$ inch, straight down, all the way around the outer outlines of the eyes. With the linoleum cutter or a chisel, scrape away the skin and $\frac{1}{4}$ to $\frac{1}{2}$ inch of flesh for the whites of the eyes, leaving the skin within the pupil outlines intact.

3 Drill two small holes into the top of each head. Insert twigs into holes to form antennae.

4 Insert a battery-operated light or an electric lightbulb inside each squash, positioning it beneath the eyes (it should sit on the interior floor of the squash).

GRIM REAPER

Bewa-a-a-re the toolshed. Someone's ready for a little skulduggery with the implement of his trade. Most butternut squashes are pear-shaped, which makes them perfect for transforming into skulls. But because butternut flesh is so thick and dense, carve with patience and extra care, working on a small section at a time.

MATERIALS

large, wide butternut squash

large screw-in hook

TOOLS

dry-erase marker

citrus zester or potter's tool

paring knife

chisel (optional)

carving knife

large spoon

drill fitted with a hole-cutter drill bit (optional)

1 Working with the stem of the squash pointing downward, to suggest neck vertebrae, lightly outline the eyes, nasal openings, and mouth with the dry-erase marker. With the citrus zester or a potter's tool, scrape away the skin and some of the flesh to define the eye sockets and pupils, as shown. Work in a circular pattern; let the edged texture of the carving show.

2 With the paring knife, carefully cut out the nasal openings; two curved and angled cuts, about 1/2 inch deep, will be enough to define each one.

3 With the paring knife or a chisel, carve the mouth, removing small sections at a time. Carve as deeply as you can.

4 Cut a door in the back near the stem end. Work patiently. Scrape out the seeds and carve until the mouth is open all the way through. Trim and neaten the edges of the mouth opening as needed.

5 Screw the hook into the crown of the skull. If you're using a thick screw hook, you may want to drill a pilot hole first to keep the squash from splitting. Hang the skull.

QUEEN OF THE CROWS

MATERIALS

1 large pumpkin

English ivy plant in plastic pot

2 lady apples

toothpicks

1 small long-necked gourd

1 red chile pepper

floral u-pins

black witch's hat and artificial crows (available from costume and party-supply stores)

tissues or newspaper

TOOLS

pencil

carving knife

large spoon

Only a sorceress as commanding as she could call these black-feathered friends to nest in her tumbling ivy tresses. Scary skin (look for an extra-warty pumpkin) superbly sets off bulging lady-apple eyeballs, a twisting gourd-stem nose, and stern hot-pepper lips. This is a (nearly) no-carve character that's fun to create with children. Consider making a coven of variations!

1 Around the stem of the pumpkin, mark a circle about the same diameter as the diameter of the top of the ivy pot. Cut out the circle. Remove seeds and pulp from the inside of the pumpkin. Fit the potted ivy into the top of the pumpkin and arrange the ivy to resemble messy hair.

2 For the eyes, attach the lady apples to the pumpkin with toothpicks. For the nose, cut the neck off the gourd and attach it with toothpicks. For the mouth, attach the pepper with toothpicks or a floral u-pin.

3 To help support the hat's pointy shape, if necessary, stuff it with crumpled tissue or newspaper. Place the witch's hat on the head and anchor it to the pumpkin with floral u-pins. Perch the crows around the witch.

MASKED GOBLIN

Not until midnight will identities be revealed! Autumn leaves of various shapes, sizes, and hues—instead of feathers and sequins—dress up a plain black mask; the black ribbon band hides the slice of the pumpkin's lid.

MATERIALS

very large, tall, bulbous pumpkin

black eye mask and black ribbon

assorted autumn leaves

floral u-pins

tall taper candle

votive candle

TOOLS

carving knife

large spoon

dry-erase marker

scissors

stapler

craft glue or hot-glue gun

fireplace matches

1 Cut a lid from the top of the pumpkin, making the cut where you want the eyes to be, and remove the seeds and the pulp. Cut a chimney vent near the top of the back side of the pumpkin.

2 Place the lid on the pumpkin. Hold the mask up to the pumpkin, eyes centered on the slice of the lid. Trace the eye holes with the dry-erase marker. Also mark the wide, grinning mouth. Cut out the top and bottom halves of the eyes from the body and lid of the pumpkin, and cut out the mouth.

3 Cut a piece of ribbon about 1½ feet longer than the circumference of the lip, cut it in half, and staple each piece to the side of the mask. Set the mask on a work surface and arrange the leaves. Glue the leaves to the mask.

4 Insert the two candles, the taper to provide light near the eyes, and the votive candle for light below the mouth.

5 Position the mask over the eye openings and attach it with floral u-pins where the ribbon meets the mask. Wrap the ribbon to the back and tie in a knot or a bow.

SCAR-FACED MONSTER

No doubt a kin of Frankenstein's infamous creature, this not-at-all-handsome fellow is a frightful assemblage of parts—including his visible brain. To make one like him, select a large, squarish pumpkin, preferably with bulges and blemishes. This jack-o'-lantern requires only the most basic carving techniques—the misshapen add-on dentures provide the special effects.

MATERIALS

1 large pumpkin

several stems of cockscomb

3 small round gourds

1 ear Indian corn, trimmed to desired length

toothpicks or bamboo skewers

candle or battery-operated light

TOOLS

carving knife

large spoon

dry-erase marker

paring knife

citrus zester or potter's tool

1 Cut a door in the back of the pumpkin and scoop out the seeds and pulp. Cut a chimney vent behind the stem near the top of the pumpkin.

2 With the dry-erase marker, sketch the eyes, nose, and mouth. Plan carefully so the round gourds will fit snugly into the eye sockets and the corn will fit into the mouth. Cut the eyes, nose, and mouth. With the citrus zester or a potter's tool, score two lines under one eye to suggest a black eye. Wedge in the gourd eyeballs. Remove several kernels from the cob to simulate missing teeth, then wedge it into the mouth opening.

3 Mark and cut a hole on one side of the forehead to accommodate the cockscomb "brains" snugly. Trim the stems from the cockscomb, then wedge the bunch into place.

4 For ears, cut the third gourd into quarters; clean out two of them. Insert two toothpicks into one cut edge of each "ear"; attach both to the head. Trim the toothpicks if necessary.

5 Insert the candle or light and replace the door.

SUNNY JACK

The long, thick eyelashes and happy disposition of this cheerful spirit virtually fly in the face of any Halloween haunting. Vials of water hidden inside the pumpkin keep the sunflower blossoms perky, no matter how late the party goes; use daisies on a smaller pumpkin.

MATERIALS

1 large round pumpkin

2 sunflowers or similarly petaled flowers

2 florist's vials

votive candles or battery-operated light

TOOLS

carving knife

large spoon

dry-erase marker

paring knife

apple corer

1 Cut out a door in the back of the pumpkin and remove the seeds and the pulp. With the dry-erase marker, outline the nose and mouth and cut them out.

2 Holding the flower stem pointing downward, remove several petals from the right and left sides of each flower, leaving the remaining petals to resemble eyelashes. Hold the flowers up to the pumpkin and mark the two spots where the stems will slip into the pumpkin. With the apple corer, punch out the two holes for the stems. Cut the flower stems and slip them through the holes. Reach in through the door and slip the stems into water-filled florist's vials.

3 Insert the candles or the light and replace the door.

SCAREDY CAT

For basic jack-o'-lantern faces, all but the most timid carvers may want to freehand-sketch the outlines directly onto the pumpkin—or even carve first and think later. For more precise shapes, like this howling, yowling, meowing feline silhouette, it's best to draw the design on paper and then transfer it to the surface of the pumpkin.

MATERIALS

medium to large squarish pumpkin

candle

TOOLS

plain paper and pencil

tape

ballpoint pen or punch prick

carving knife

large spoon

paring knife

linoleum cutter or chisel

1 Sketch a cat design on paper, or photocopy the cat on the front cover of this book, enlarging the size if necessary.

2 Tape the pattern to the pumpkin. With the ballpoint pen or a punch prick, poke closely spaced holes through the outline and into the pumpkin's flesh. Remove the pattern.

3 Cut a door in the back of the pumpkin. Scrape out the seeds and the pulp.

4 Cut out the cat outline, connecting the dots.

5 For the standing-on-end hairs: Cut some hairs with the linoleum cutter or a chisel, going only part of the way into the flesh; cut others by making two closely angled cuts with a paring knife, cutting all the way through.

6 Insert the candle and replace the back door.

CREEPY SPIDER AND WEB

MATERIALS

large pumpkin

small pumpkin

candles or battery-operated lights

TOOLS

carving knife

large spoon

3/4-inch masking tape

linoleum cutter or chisel

dry-erase marker

narrow knife or keyhole saw

fireplace matches

It will certainly take some time, but this intricate spiderweb is actually quite easy to carve. Once you've marked the pattern with masking tape, cut and chisel everything that's not the web, leaving a thin layer of golden flesh to glow. Carve a creepy-crawly spider on another pumpkin, and the unsightly scene is set.

1 Cut a door in the back of each pumpkin. Scrape out the seeds and the pulp. Cut a vent hole behind the stem of each pumpkin.

2 With the masking tape, make a cross that covers the face of the larger pumpkin, then make the same sized X over the cross. Make concentric octagons that connect the arms of the web with smaller lengths of tape.

3 Using the linoleum cutter or a chisel, cut and chisel away the areas of flesh between the tape, leaving about 1/4 to 1/2 inch of flesh. Remove the tape.

4 For the spider, mark the outline on the front of the smaller pumpkin with the dry-erase marker. Use the narrow knife or a saw to cut out the design; carve all the way through the pumpkin.

5 Set candles or lights in both pumpkins and replace the back doors. You will probably need several candles to illuminate the spiderweb; if it does not glow sufficiently, scrape away more of the flesh from the inside, being careful not to make a hole in the panels of the web.

Score Yourself Some Pumpkins

These **artistically inscribed pumpkins** will prove once and for all that beauty is skin deep. Achieve these enchanting effects by scoring the skin of any pumpkin with a linoleum cutter rather than cutting all the way through. Design motifs and inspiration can come from fine art or pop culture, wallpaper or other textiles, or simply from your imagination. **Let the pumpkin be your canvas!** When the pumpkin is illuminated, the subtle glow will only add to the artistry. **Tip:** To keep the exposed flesh fresh-looking for a party, rub a coating of Vaseline over it, then wipe it off before the event.

ABOVE, FROM LEFT TO RIGHT: **A poncho bordered in bright, simple leaf appliqués was the inspiration for this fall-foliage–themed pumpkin. The Cinderella pumpkin, center, has deep reddish orange skin and bright orange flesh that dramatically evokes the fabric beneath it. The curliques on the pumpkin on the right were inspired by the curly motif on the dining room walls.** OPPOSITE PAGE: **The thorny vines on this antique transferware platter suggested the delicate design inscribed on this Blue Hubbard squash.**

QUILTED PUMPKINS

MATERIALS

Lumina pumpkins

TOOLS

dry-erase marker

paring knife

linoleum cutter or chisel

Look around the house: A quilt, a vintage printed tablecloth, or a wallpaper border could be your inspiration. This pair of country classics features positive/negative motifs borrowed from antique quilts. The designs are chiseled only into the surface, so these sophisticated table decorations are long-lasting.

1 For these designs, a checkerboard pattern repeats around the pumpkin, alternating in a positive/negative image. With the dry-erase marker, mark three parallel lines, evenly spaced around the circumference of each pumpkin. Draw evenly spaced vertical lines from the top line to the bottom line to create a series of squares.

2 For the smaller, diamond motif, use the paring knife to cut a diamond from one square, then, on the next square, cut out the space around a diamond. Cut deeply enough to reveal the pattern, but no deeper. Continue, alternating, all the way around the pumpkin.

3 For the larger, floral motif, draw a petal within each square, alternating the diagonal orientation. Use the linoleum cutter or a chisel to scrape away a petal or the area surrounding a petal, alternating square by square. Cut deeply enough to reveal the pattern, but no deeper.

FALLING AUTUMN LEAVES

MATERIALS

medium to large squash

assorted leaves

TOOLS

plain paper and pencil

tape

scissors

ballpoint pen or punch prick

linoleum cutter or chisel

Gather a collection of shapely leaves from the yard, a park, or the woods—maple, oak, and beech, for example—and use them as templates for this delicately tooled work of art. The technique, in fact, can be applied to almost any pumpkin, squash, or gourd. Use your results as a lunch-table centerpiece, a porch-bench decoration, or a gift for a neighbor.

1 Trace the outlines of the leaves onto the paper. Cut out a rectangle surrounding each leaf outline, so you can position and trace each pattern individually.

2 Select the placement for one leaf at a time on the pumpkin and tape it into place. Use the ballpoint pen or a punch prick to trace over the leaf outline, scoring it into the surface of the pumpkin. Remove the paper and repeat with the other leaf outlines all around the pumpkin. You'll probably want to repeat the same outline several times on the same pumpkin.

3 With the linoleum cutter or a chisel, carve the leaf outlines into the flesh, going over each outline only once. Add lines to mimic the actual veins on the leaves.

Preserve Your Pumpkin

A pumpkin that has a design carved into its surface but isn't hollowed out will last longer than a traditional jack-o'-lantern. If you're saving sugar pumpkins for pies or soups, they can still become little monsters for Halloween: Tip them on their sides and gouge out two eyes and a mouth around the stem nose (see Pumpkins with Personality, page 23). Some carvers suggest rubbing a jack-o'-lantern's cut edge with a little petroleum jelly to seal in moisture. To rehydrate a slightly shriveled one, soak it in water for a few hours.

STYLISH GOURD LANTERNS

The sliver-shaped windows ringing these lanterns perfectly frame the flames inside. Set them anywhere you'd normally use votive candles—a row down the center of a dinner table, a group on an entry-hall console, or one on a bathroom vanity. Set a coordinating saucer beneath each one for a decorative flourish—and to protect surfaces.

1 Cut a circle that's a bit larger than a votive candle from the bottom of each gourd and discard the circle. With a sturdy soup spoon, a grapefruit spoon, or an iced tea spoon, scrape out the seeds and the pulp.

2 With a dry-erase marker, draw vertical sliver-shaped windows at even intervals around the gourd; adjust the proportions of the windows to complement the size and shape of each gourd. Cut out the shapes. (After you've cut out each window, you may want to trim their sides, angling the side walls outward to create wider openings for the light.)

3 Set a votive candle on each plate or saucer and place the gourd lantern over it.

MATERIALS

small to medium lantern-shaped gourds

votive candles

small plates or saucers

TOOLS

carving knife

soup spoon, grapefruit spoon, or iced tea spoon

dry-erase marker

paring knife

FAUX PINEAPPLE FINIALS

The gesture is real, but the symbols are an illusion. Pineapples, representing bounty and hospitality, are often depicted in carved-wood finials on furniture and fence posts. This pair of pumpkins masquerade as pineapples to beckon visitors along a path sculpted of autumn leaves. Boxwood clippings serve as the fronds.

MATERIALS

2 pineapple-shaped pumpkins

boxwood or other evergreen branches

floral wire

sheet moss or sphagnum moss

battery-operated lights or outdoor-approved light sockets with 25- to 40-watt bulbs

TOOLS

carving knife

large spoon

3/4-inch masking tape

linoleum cutter or chisel

paring knife

1 Cut a door in the back of each pumpkin. Cut a chimney vent behind each stem. Scoop out the seeds and the pulp.

2 With the masking tape, mark a cross-hatch design on the front and sides of each pumpkin, as shown above. Cut straight into the flesh of the pumpkin, about 1/2 inch deep (not all the way through), along the edges of the tape. Remove the tape.

3 With the linoleum cutter or a chisel, chisel and scrape out the channels that were under the tape, being careful not to carve all the way through.

4 In the middle of each diamond, carve a small downward-pointing triangle. Cut deep, but not all the way through.

5 For the fronds, secure two bundles of boxwood clippings together with floral wire. Cut a hole in the top of each pumpkin to hold each bundle. Wrap the base of each bundle with moss for a soft finish, and insert the greens.

6 Put the lights into the pumpkins and replace the back doors. Scrape more flesh from the inside, if needed, to allow the light to show through.

POLKA-DOT PUMPKINS

MATERIALS

pumpkins

candles

TOOLS

carving knife

large spoon

apple corer or a drill fitted with a hole-cutter drill bit

Whatever you do, don't connect these dots. Repetition is the name of the game. You can be a little formal and work a swagged design to echo antique upholstery-tack patterns. Or follow a loping curve, zigzag, or a perfectly straight line around the circumference. This is one way to carve a lot of pumpkins very quickly—without mistakes!

1 Cut a door and a chimney vent in the back of the pumpkin. Scoop out the seeds and the pulp.

2 With the apple corer or a drill fitted with a hole-cutter bit, create a "garland" of holes around the pumpkin, spacing them as evenly as possible. Make the holes in a scallop pattern or a gentle wave, as desired. Add a hole (or holes) on the door.

3 Put the candle inside the pumpkin and replace the door.

Pairing Off

If one is good, two must be better. Pairs of identical jack-o'-lanterns flanking a doorway, sideboard, mantel, or front gate always make an elegant statement. Another option is to devise a duo of complementary designs. Some suggestions: a cat and a mouse, easy-to-execute patterns of circles and squares, a flying bat and a crescent moon, the outlines of a standing coffin and tombstone, and an acorn and an oak leaf.

FLAME, FLICKER, AND GLOW

Before lighting the first real fire of the cold-weather months, outfit the hearth with pumpkins carved to resemble licks of flame. For a more pronounced effect, put more than one candle in each pumpkin. To build a bigger arrangement, set one or more pumpkins atop improvised risers of wide, flat pumpkins.

MATERIALS

several tall pumpkins

candles

TOOLS

carving knife

large spoon

dry-erase marker

linoleum cutter or potter's tool

1 Cut a door in the back of each pumpkin. Cut a chimney vent behind each stem.

2 With the dry-erase marker, draw flame shapes on the front of the pumpkins. Begin by carefully carving away only the outline of the flame, being sure to leave the base of each flame attached.

3 With the linoleum cutter or a potter's tool, cut lines in the flesh within each flame just deeply enough to add flickering details, as shown in the photo, opposite. You may want to reach in through the back door with your noncarving hand to steady the flame and keep it from breaking off as you add these details.

4 Put candles inside the pumpkins and replace the doors.

[CHAPTER TWO]

enchanting handmade decorations

deck your home with gourds and ghosts

When it comes to decorating for Halloween, whether for a grand party or for simply scaring the neighborhood goblins, look to the icons of the holiday for inspiration. Their simple shapes are instantly recognizable: a carved pumpkin, a witch on a broom, a black cat, a flying bat, a giant spider. These are the stuff of costumes, cutouts for windows, party invitations, even cookies. To set the stage for your Halloween house, start with the jack-o'-lantern, the most enduring Halloween symbol of all and the beacon that guides trick-or-treaters to the house where a welcome is waiting.

The traditional produce of fall can be a large part of decorating for Halloween, whether you live in the city or miles from civilization. Indian corn, gourds, pumpkins, and other fall vegetables from a farmers' market are so evocative that they can become a simple, beautiful centerpiece, mantelpiece, or porch still-life with little or no adornment—witness the Shades of Fall Topiary on page 62. Sheaves of cornstalks attached to fence posts and porch railings, though today seen as merely decorative, actually represent the coming of winter and all that Halloween originally stood for.

The most exciting thing about fixing up your home for Halloween is that so many ideas can be executed with things found around the house (be sure to look in the basement, garage, and attic). Leaves, branches, and a rake; clothes from an old chest in the attic; cardboard boxes, tin cans, and broom sticks—all can add to your Halloween decorating plans. Even a haunted house can be created with everyday things from the pantry (think cold cooked spaghetti, globs of gelatin). Once the lights are dimmed, people's imaginations go a long way.

Outside, don't make it too easy for the little goblins to demand their treats: Create a mystery by illuminating the pathway to the house with a ghostly glow—small carved pumpkins or paper bags block-printed with skeletons (see photo, page 65), all giving off flickering candle light. Or turn the yard into a creepy setup for whatever waits on the other side of the door: A well-situated tree is just where ghosts like to hang out. If there's not a convenient tree, drape a white sheet over a pumpkin set atop two bales of hay. Sheets or large white pieces of construction paper cut in ghostly shapes and tacked over windows will fill all who approach with apprehension, especially when the only light inside comes from a candle (not too close to sheets or paper, please).

All Hallows' Eve Atmosphere

Consider these other ideas for bringing the spirit of Halloween to your home:

* Create an arrangement of hollowed-out crown-of-thorn squash and bottleneck gourds to **hold candles.**

* Cornhusks and branches with autumn leaves and berries or dangling apples **celebrate the harvest season** and are fetching hung on doors and around mantels.

* Moss, spread out with fall-colored leaves, makes a fitting centerpiece on a serving table. Hollowed-out cabbages, pumpkins, and turnips are **fun vessels for Halloween treats**.

* Arrange tall bare branches in pots strategically placed around the room—they'll look like **spooky "skeleton hands"** reaching out.

* **Fake spiderwebs** make everything appear musty and old. For instant creepiness, pull them around bare tree branches, a musty thrift shop portrait in a distressed frame, or a junk shop candelabra.

* Glue-gun fall leaves or cutouts of ghosts, skeletons, and witches onto sheer black fabric and hang in a doorway to **create a dramatic entrance** to a haunted room.

* And that **old-fashioned broom** in the corner—was it left by a guest or...?

HARVEST WREATH

MATERIALS

ornamental grasses

oak leaves

rosehips

twine (if needed for drying)

spool of waxed floral wire

square Styrofoam wreath base or picture frame

picture hangers

thick ribbon (optional)

This bewitching autumn wreath can be crafted with items from your yard, a farm stand, or even the supermarket. Let readily-available seasonal materials be your guide.

1 If your grasses and leaves are fresh and green, you'll need to dry them. Tie them in bundles with twine and hang them upside-down in a dark, dry place, such as the attic or garage, for 7 to 10 days.

2 Tie the end of the spool of floral wire to the wreath base. Use an overhand wrapping motion as you unwind the wire to attach bunches of dried grasses, leaves, and rosehips to the base.

3 After working your way around the entire base, pause to adjust the natural materials for full coverage and an attractive composition. Use picture hangers and, if you like, a thick ribbon to hang the finished wreath on your front door or in the entryway.

Harvest Centerpiece

Make a matching centerpiece for your dining table: Substitute a small square or circular Styrofoam wreath for the large one. Add an orange or gold pillar candle in the middle to complete the look.

SHADES OF FALL TOPIARY

MATERIALS

a variety of flattish pumpkins

long wooden dowel

garden urn filled with soil or sand

toothpicks or bamboo skewers

hardy greenery, such as the leafy top of a brussels sprout stalk or other autumn leafy greens

TOOLS

carving knife

large spoon

drill fitted with a hole-cutter drill bit

saw

The harvest of autumn squashes yields so many subtle, distinctive colors: bluish grays, frosted taupes, milky whites. It's easy to go a little overboard at the farm stand when you come across a gorgeous array. If you choose varieties that are fairly flat, stacking is enough to transform them into artful displays.

1 Gently break off the stems of the pumpkins to be used in the tower. Decide on your stacking order.

2 For the topmost pumpkin, cut off the top and scoop out the seeds and pulp.

3 Reserve the pumpkin destined for the top. Drill a dowel-diameter hole straight down through the center of each pumpkin's top; turn over each pumpkin and drill the same size hole straight down the bottom center until you drill through to the top hole. Using the saw, cut the dowel to the height of the tower plus the depth of the urn. Insert the dowel into the soil or sand in the urn and press to make it secure. Slide each pumpkin down the dowel (you may need to wiggle each one as you line up the holes and then wipe away any seeds and pulp that are pressed out during the process). Attach the hollowed-out pumpkin to the top pumpkin with three or four toothpicks or pieces of skewer. Fill this vase with the greenery.

SKELETON LUMINARIAS

In the Southwest, luminarias—paper bags filled with sand anchoring a candle—are placed along a path to guide visitors. On Halloween, the familiar brown-paper bags take on a slightly sinister quality as they lead small gremlins or dinner guests to the front door. When you set the bags out, position them along the walkway where they will not be knocked over and be sure they are completely open to prevent them from burning.

MATERIALS

black water-soluble block-printing ink, such as Speedball

12½- by 6-inch brown paper bags

sand

3-inch-tall votive candles in glass containers

TOOLS

Styrofoam trays (used for packing foods—ask your butcher for clean, unused trays or thoroughly wash used ones)

X-Acto knife

cuticle stick or any hard-tipped instrument, such as tip of paint brush handle, end of spoon, or dull pencil (to trace patterns in the Styrofoam)

windowpane-size piece of glass or acrylic

6- to 8-inch-wide brayer (ink roller available in art supply stores)

large spoon

1 Cut the Styrofoam trays to 4- by 8-inch rectangles so they lie flat. With the cuticle stick, draw designs into the Styrofoam. This is a reverse process. The design you draw will be part of the non-inked part of the bag, and it will be a mirror image of the print.

2 Squeeze about 1½ inches of ink onto the glass. Roll the brayer back and forth to spread the ink (it may be sticky at first). Once the brayer is covered with an even coat of ink, roll it across a Styrofoam image.

3 Press the side of a brown paper bag onto the Styrofoam. Rub the paper bag with a large serving spoon, pressing the paper into the Styrofoam with a back and forth movement.

4 Carefully remove the bag and set it aside to dry (approximately 10 minutes). Reink the Styrofoam or use another piece with a different image and repeat the process with additional bags.

5 Open the bags and fill each 1 inch deep with sand. Light the candles in their glasses and ease them into the center of the sand in the bags.

TISSUE PAPER GHOSTS

Ghosts have been a part of Halloween since it began. In ancient times, people believed that the souls or spirits of departed ones came back at this time of year to visit the living—and not always with the best intentions! Ghosts are also thought to appear to whisper of something the future holds. These lively little ghosts dance in a window, foretelling the fun and treats that are about to happen!

MATERIALS

white tissue paper

white thread

**white hole reinforcers
(from office supply stores)**

TOOLS

oak tag

pencil

small craft scissors

medium hole punch

small hole punch

1 To make patterns, draw simple ghosts on the oak tag and cut them out.

2 Place the patterns on a piece of tissue paper and trace around them. With the craft scissors, carefully cut out the ghosts.

3 With the medium hole punch, make eyes. With the small hole punch, make one hole at the top of each head. Pull various lengths of thread through the small hole and knot.

4 Attach the hole reinforcers to the ends of the threads and hang the ghosts on the window mullion. Trim excess thread.

Spooky Special Effects

To make your windows even scarier, paint spooky swirls on the glass. Line the window sash with masking tape before you begin. Mix ½ tablespoon of white powdered tempera with 1 tablespoon clear dishwashing soap to a creamy consistency in a foil muffin tin (or use a product called Glass Wax, available in hardware stores). Apply to the window glass in ghostly swirls with a slightly damp sponge or paper towel. To remove the dried paint, simply rub off with a dry paper towel.

FRONT-DOOR SCARECROW

This funny fellow will greet visitors from Halloween through Thanksgiving. Children will love collecting the elements that make up his attire, from the old clothes to the colorful fall leaves.

MATERIALS

large bamboo rake with wooden pole

24-inch branch, approximately the same diameter as the rake pole

$\frac{1}{2}$- by $\frac{1}{8}$-inch bolt with nut

branch, approximately 1$\frac{1}{2}$ inch diameter

small gourd

1-inch drywall screw

green twine

leaves

bittersweet

old shirt, overalls, gloves, bandana, and boots

TOOLS

drill with $\frac{1}{8}$-inch drill bit

saw

hammer and 1$\frac{1}{2}$-inch nails

sharp knife (if needed)

wide-head scewdriver (optional)

1 For the arms, with the $\frac{1}{8}$-inch drill bit, drill a hole, front to back, through the pole of the rake, 6 inches down from the neck. Drill another $\frac{1}{8}$-inch hole through the middle of the 24-inch branch. Place the branch over the pole, matching the holes. Insert the bolt and tighten with the nut. You can now rotate the arms into a perpendicular position.

2 For the eyes, cut two $\frac{3}{4}$-inch slices from the remaining branch with the saw. Hammer a nail into the center of each slice to create the pupil of the eye (you may want to drill a hole first to prevent any splitting). The nail should stick out beyond the wood in the back. This will be used to wedge the eyes in place between the bamboo prongs.

3 For the nose, hold the gourd firmly and take off any stem that remains (or use the saw or sharp knife to cut it off). Screw the drywall screw partially into where you have removed the stem, leaving $\frac{1}{2}$ inch of the screw exposed. The head of the screw can then be slid into place and wedged between the prongs of the rake, as with the eyes. (It may help to use a wide-head screwdriver to separate the prongs of the rake).

4 For the mouth, cut 2 lengths of twine and twist together. Slip them into position in between the prongs of the rake.

5 Weave leaves and bittersweet or other vines in between the prongs of the rake for hair. Dress the scarecrow with the shirt, overalls, gloves, and bandana. Tie two 4-foot pieces of twine to the overall straps in the back, thread one piece down each pant leg, then tie on the boots.

SPOOK-TACULAR PAPER GARLANDS

MATERIALS

orange, white, and black lightweight paper, 36 inches wide

TOOLS

construction paper and pencil

small craft scissors and X-Acto knife

needle and thread

No self-respecting haunted house would be caught "dead" without bats, black cats, jack-o'-lanterns, and at least a few ghosts to create a scary atmosphere. Fun and easy-to-make, these festive garlands can be hung just about everywhere—in doorways, across the mantel, or along the edge of a table. Store them carefully and you will be able to use them for many Halloweens to come.

1 With a photocopier, enlarge the bat, cat, ghost, and pumpkin templates on page 214 by 200 percent (or design patterns of your own). With the templates, make patterns from the construction paper.

2 Cut a 36-inch strip from the orange lightweight paper. Fold, accordion style, with each panel the same width as the pumpkin pattern. Trace the pumpkin on the first panel, making sure the pattern touches both right and left folded edges.

3 Cut through all the folded strip layers, being sure that you don't cut off all of the folded edges. Use the X-Acto knife to cut out eyes and mouth. Unfold. With the needle and thread, thread a piece of string to each end of the cutout.

4 Repeat with bat, cat, and ghost designs on different-colored strips of paper.

BOO-TIFUL
BLOCK-PRINT INVITATIONS

Invite your friends to a Halloween party with these bold cards that set the tone for the event, or send them as holiday greeting cards. The pumpkin invitation at left in the photo is created by a block-printing process, a technique that makes it easy to create a large quantity of cards. Instructions for the other two invites are on the following pages.

Instructions for the other two invites are on the following pages.

1 For each invitation, cut a rectangle of orange paper about 10 by 3 inches. Trim one short edge with the scallop scissors. Fold in half crosswise, so that the scallop edge is a bit longer than the other.

2 Trim the printing block so that it is slightly smaller than the folded pieces of paper. With a pencil, lightly draw your design onto the block. This is a reverse process: The lines you draw will be the non-inked part of the invitation, and the print will be a mirror image of what you draw. Using the linoleum cutter tool and blade, cut out the design (children should be able to do this with the help of an adult).

3 Squeeze a quarter-size blob of ink onto the glass. Roll the brayer back and forth to spread the ink (it may be sticky at first). Once the brayer is covered with an even coat of ink, roll it across the printing block.

4 Center and carefully place the front side of the invitation onto the inked block. Without shifting it, rub the paper hard, then peel away. Repeat with the remaining invitations, reinking the block each time.

MATERIALS

orange construction paper

black water-soluble block-printing ink, such as Speedball

TOOLS

X-Acto knife

metal-edged ruler

scallop-edged scissors

rubber printing block, such as Speedy Cut from Speedball

pencil

linoleum cutter tool and blade (available at art supply stores)

windowpane-size piece of glass or acrylic

brayer (ink roller available at art supply stores)

SLASH-AND-PASTE "BOO" INVITATIONS

Try a simple rhyming verse written on the inside of the invitation to tell the tale of your party's time, date, place, and costume theme. These invitations can also be made with blank store-bought cards, embellished with the cutouts.

1 For each invitation, cut a rectangle of white paper about 4 by 5 inches. Fold in half crosswise to make a 4- by 2½-inch card. Trim the short edges with the zigzag scissors.

2 Cut a rectangle of black paper slightly smaller than 4 by 2½ inches. With the white pencil, write your message (in this case the word *BOO*) lightly on the center of the paper and cut out with the X-Acto knife (don't worry about the insides of the letters yet). Discard the letters and apply glue stick to surrounding black. Center on the white folded card.

3 With the hole punch, punch out 4 black dots for the insides of the letters. Glue stick the dots in place, using tweezers to help handle the pieces.

SLASH-AND-PASTE PUMPKIN INVITATIONS

MATERIALS

orange construction paper

black construction paper

green twine

TOOLS

X-Acto knife

metal-edged ruler

zigzag- or scallop-edged scissors

glue stick

craft glue

tweezers

This card is another example of the many different designs that can be created with boldly colored paper and a pair of decorative scissors. Vary your design according to the kind of party you are having—depending on the paper and design you choose, this can be made to the height of sophistication or to please any child. Bats, witches, cats—any graphic shape will work, and you can adapt the size of the card to fit your design.

1 For each invitation, cut a rectangle of orange paper about 12 by 5 inches. Fold in half crosswise to make a 6- by 5-inch card. Trim the short edges with the zigzag scissors.

2 Cut a rectangle of black paper slightly smaller than 6 by 5 inches. Cut out a moon on the upper right portion of the card with the X-Acto knife. Apply glue from the glue stick to the underside of the black paper and center on the folded orange paper. Trim any excess overhang with the X-Acto knife and ruler.

3 Cut out three 2-inch circles from the orange paper for the pumpkins. Apply glue from the glue stick and place on the invitation. From the black paper, cut out facial features and glue them in place on the pumpkins, using tweezers to help handle the tiny pieces.

4 Cut 3 short lengths of green twine. Glue to the top of the pumpkins with craft glue.

PLAYFUL PAINTED TABLECLOTH

MATERIALS

42-inch square white cotton sheeting

textile medium

orange, yellow, and black acrylic paint

20 packages orange, black, and white jumbo rickrack

TOOLS

fabric glue, such as Fabri-Tac

orange and yellow colored pencils

brushes

Bring out this tablecloth every year to set a festive Halloween mood. Painting images on black fabric would make for a moodier and scarier backdrop to a buffet feast. You could also make matching cotton napkins, repeating an icon from the tablecloth in a corner of each napkin.

1 Turn the sheeting under ¼ inch on all 4 sides. Press and glue down with the fabric glue.

2 With the colored pencils, lightly mark pumpkin, moon, and star designs on the cloth. For each color, mix together equal parts textile medium and paint. Paint the shapes and outline loosely with black.

3 Cut the rickrack into 4½-inch strips. Alternating colors, glue one end of each strip to the turned-in edges of the cloth. Let dry.

4 With machine stitching, top stitch along the edge of the cloth, securing the rickrack.

SPOOKY FELT PILLOWS

It doesn't take witchcraft to make these, just simple sewing skill.

MATERIALS

two 15-inch pillow forms or two 1-pound bags of polyester fiberfill

1 yard paper-backed fusible web, such as HeatnBond Ultra Hold

2 yards black felt

2 yards orange felt

20 inches Velcro sew-on tape

TOOLS

ballpoint pen

scissors

¾ yard contact paper

X-Acto knife

metal-edged ruler

straight pins

fabric glue (optional)

1 With a photocopier, enlarge the cat, moon, and star template by 425% (see page 214) and transfer or trace it onto the backing of the fusible web. Iron to a piece of black felt and cut out shapes. From the orange felt, cut out one 15½-inch square for the front and two 15½- by 9-inch rectangles for the back.

2 To make the borders, iron a 15- by 3-inch piece of fusible web to a 15- by 3-inch piece of black felt. Remove the backing and iron to another piece of black felt (sandwiching the adhesive between 2 layers of felt). On a 15- by 3-inch strip of contact paper, draw 7 connecting triangles, each about 2½ inches at the base. Cut out with the X-Acto knife and ruler. Attach the contact paper template to the felt and cut along the edges. Peel off the contact paper. Press down any fuzz pick-up with a hot iron. Repeat to make 3 more borders. Place the borders along each side of the front orange square, points facing in. Baste in position.

3 Turn one long edge of a back piece 1 inch and press. Center and pin one side of a 10-inch Velcro strip along this edge and sew it in place with 2 parallel lines. Attach the other side of the Velcro strip in the same place on the second back felt piece. Remove the pins.

4 Press the Velcro strips together to make one closed back. Pin this piece to the front square, right sides together and border pieces on the inside. Trim the back, if necessary, to the same size as the front. With a ¼-inch seam allowance, sew front to back along three sides. Remove the pins and trim the seams. Turn right side out.

5 Insert a magazine inside the pillow cover. Remove the backing from the black shapes and iron to the pillow front. Add fabric glue to any pieces that don't adhere. Stuff the pillow with a pillow form or fiberfill. Glue the open back edges on the sides of the Velcro closed.

6 Repeat with the pumpkin design (see template, page 214) to make a black pillow with an orange cutout.

CANDY CORN PLACEHOLDERS

MATERIALS

2 ½-inch-tall terra-cotta flower pots

white, yellow, and orange acrylic

orange construction paper

cellophane wrap

candy corn and other Halloween candy

orange pipe cleaners

TOOLS

sponge brushes

zigzag-edged scissors

hole punch

black ink pen

small craft scissors

pencil

Give your guests something to take home besides the shivers! For a sit-down dinner, place one of these at each place setting, or, at a more informal gathering, have a tray (lined with fall leaves, sphagnum moss, or black felt) of these goodie-filled painted pots waiting by the door for your friends to grab as they leave the party.

1 With a sponge brush, paint the inside and outside of each pot with one coat of white paint. Let dry.

2 Paint a ½-inch stripe of yellow paint around the bottom edge of each pot. Let dry. Paint a 1½-inch orange stripe above the yellow stripe of each pot, going a little bit up into the rim. Let dry. Paint another coat of white paint around the top ½ inch of the rim of each pot. Let dry.

3 With the zigzag scissors, cut tags out of the orange paper. Punch a hole in the upper left corner and write a name on each.

4 Cut 10-inch squares of cellophane. Place some candy in the center of each and gather the sides up around the candy. Twist a pipe cleaner around each to gather. Thread one end of each pipe cleaner through a tag and then coil the ends by wrapping around a pencil. Place the candy bags inside the pots.

MINI-PUMPKIN PLACECARDS

MATERIALS

very small sugar and/or Jack Be Little pumpkins

garden twine

TOOLS

dry-erase marker

citrus zester or linoleum cutter

scissors

Carve a personalized coat of arms or a simple rendering of initials on a miniature pumpkin for every guest at an autumn dinner party. This is a sweet touch for the Thanksgiving table, of course, but for a frightful Halloween alternative, surround the initials with a tombstone outline and, to be extra wicked, add "R.I.P."

1 If you're using a very small sugar pumpkin, as shown opposite, use a dry-erase marker to draw initials and a frame (we used a shield shape) on the pumpkin. With a citrus zester or a linoleum cutter, cut out the letters and the frame.

2 If you're using a Jack Be Little, draw one initial into each of the ridges. This variety of pumpkin can be quite hard, so it's best to carve with a linoleum cutter.

3 For a tassel, tie a piece of natural or green garden twine around each stem, use scissors to trim it to desired length, and fray the ends.

Writing Class

If you're feeling eloquent, put your pumpkin to work as a writing tablet. Wielding a zester or a linoleum cutter instead of a pen, you can inscribe a message to a friend, scrawl spooky words for a Halloween display ("Beware!" "Trick-or-Treat!" "Boo!"), or create a holiday greeting card to deliver to a neighbor's doorstep.

cheddar
corn bread
rosemary
chicken
lemon mustard
brussel sprouts

HALLOWEEN BUFFET MENU BANNERS

MATERIALS

medium gourds

6-inch bamboo skewers

colored vellum or other stiff paper

TOOLS

awl and hammer

scissors

markers

⅛-inch hole punch

Identify the dishes of a fall potluck dinner or an All Hallows' Eve buffet with hand-lettered signposts rising from colorful gourds. Use the same assemblage to list the names and prices of goodies at a bake sale or to hold table numbers at a fall wedding reception. Use colored vellum for the most luminous banners.

1   Select one gourd for each dish on your buffet table. Decide how you want to arrange the gourd, making sure that it will remain stable. Leaving the gourd in that position, pierce it once with the awl at what is now the top, tapping gently with a hammer if necessary. Push the sharp end of a skewer into the hole in the gourd.

2   Cut out vellum or paper rectangles approximately 2½ inches by 4 inches and write the name of one dish in the center of each. With the hole punch, make one hole above and one below the dish name. Slide each card onto a skewer.

Pumpkins as Art

That a pumpkin was responsible for transporting Cinderella from a life of misery to one of royal pleasure should come as no surprise. Each gourd, squash, and pumpkin in the genus *Cucurbita* possesses its own **dignified, if quirky, personality** and the power to fill a room with equal parts **humor and beauty**. This autumn, explore the pumpkin as art—you'll be amazed by the variety of shapes, sizes, colors, and textures. Presented alone or in groups, they're certain to transport you—as they did Cinderella—someplace charming.

ABOVE, FROM LEFT TO RIGHT: Resembling plump pillows or regal turbans, these Baby Boo pumpkins possess a playful majesty. Even without its grinning visage, the jack-o'-lantern pumpkin is iconic. So raise it high, as we've done here, center, and pay homage to its timeless form. The towering display on the right stems from an Australian Crown Prince pumpkin base, which is topped with a scarlet maxima pumpkin known for its brilliant rind. OPPOSITE PAGE: Texture is emphasized in a still life that marries red maple leaves and tarnished silver with warty ornamental gourds.

PUMPKIN-PATCH WREATH

MATERIALS

16- to 18-inch grapevine
wreath form

sheet moss or sphagnum
moss

fine-gauge green floral wire
or hot-glue gun

toothpicks or bamboo
skewers

5 or 6 little pumpkins or
gourds

glass hurricane lamp and
pillar candle

One of the great country pleasures is without doubt the magical afternoon search for just the right treasures in a great big pumpkin patch. Here, the strange beauty of one of those vine-filled fields is tidied and tweaked in an elegant autumn centerpiece. And unlike a vase of flowers, this arrangement will last for many weeks.

1 With the wreath form lying flat on a work surface, cover the entire top of the form with moss, securing it with lengths of floral wire (position bits of moss over the wire to obscure it). Alternatively, attach the moss to the form with hot glue.

2 Insert two toothpicks or cut pieces of bamboo skewer (no longer than the thickness of the wreath form) into the bottom of each pumpkin. Spacing the pumpkins evenly around the top of the wreath, press each one into place, anchoring the toothpicks or skewers into the vines of the form (you may need to wiggle them into place).

3 Position the wreath on the table. Place some moss inside the hurricane lamp, add the candle, and place it in the center of the wreath.

Instant Impact

With a little extra thought and planning at the farm stand or market, you can select an array of gourds and pumpkins to display as carefully as you would compose a flower arrangement. Buy small green, green-and-white, and white gourds, then group them by color on a three-tiered dessert stand. Or, for a subtle infusion of elegance, choose exclusively white gourds, including Lumina and Baby Boo pumpkins.

AUTUMN BOUQUET IN A SQUASH VASE

MATERIALS

large, upright squash or pumpkin with a level base

stalks of ornamental kale

branches of autumn leaves

branches of seeded eucalyptus

plate or platter

TOOLS

carving knife

large spoon

With the top trimmed off and the insides scooped out, a generously sized autumn squash becomes a natural vase that's completely integral to the arrangement. Splashes of purple—here, stalks of ornamental kale—freshen the expected seasonal palette of green, gold, and orange. A tableau of squash flowerpots (see photo, page 59) makes a charming seasonal display, too. Choose a variety of gourds and flowers for interest.

1. Cut across 3 or 4 inches from the top of the squash, slicing straight across. Scoop out the seeds and the pulp. Rinse out the inside and fill with water.

2. Create the arrangement: Begin with the kale, since its stalks are thicker than the other materials, then add the autumn branches, and finish with the eucalyptus, adjusting until you are satisfied with the proportion and fullness of the bouquet. To protect furniture, set the vase on a plate or platter.

Flower Arranging 101

Coordinate the materials of your arrangement with your pumpkin or gourd vase. For example, a bold orange pumpkin might hold branches of flame-colored leaves, tawny Indian corn with the husks pulled back like petals, red and orange dahlias, and bittersweet. To ensure watertightness, you can line the pumpkin with a plastic container; insert floral foam if you want to anchor a tightly composed bouquet.

GOURD-TOPPED CANDELABRA

With a little imagination, you can use a wide, flat pumpkin as the base for a dramatic and stylish candlelit centerpiece. A creamy colored specimen and a cascading pile of snow-white gourds hint at the approaching winter holiday season. To further dress the house for the season, try setting a gourd on top of every candlestick (see photo below).

1 Carefully break or cut the stem off the pumpkin. Using a bit that's just a fraction smaller than the diameter of the candles, drill five evenly spaced holes in a ring around the top of the pumpkin, drilling straight down 1 or 2 inches.

2 Insert the candles into the holes; scrape the openings a tiny bit if necessary. If the holes are too big, secure the candle by wrapping the base with a strip of plastic wrap or a small amount of modeling glue.

3 Arrange the greenery on top of the pumpkin, allowing it to trail down the sides, and secure it in place with floral u-pins. Arrange the gourds on top of the greenery, securing each gourd to the pumpkin with a toothpick, if necessary, for stability. Set several gourds on the table, around the base of the pumpkin, to enhance the cascading effect.

SQUASH CANDLE MOLDS

MATERIALS

acorn and Hubbard squash (and others, if available)

bee's wax or regular paraffin candle wax (allow about ½ pound for each candle)

yellow, orange, coral, and/or purple wax color tablets

candle wicks

wick tabs

TOOLS

carving knife

large spoon

melon baller

double boiler

scissors

pencil

Fill a room with candlelight and it sets the stage for a cozy evening. Candles can be made at home quite easily, and using small winter squash as molds creates graceful shapes. Choose different-color tablets to tint the wax in a range of harvest tones.

1 Cut the tops off the squash and hollow out the insides. (For Hubbard squash, scrape out the seeds with a large spoon. For acorn, use the melon baller to scoop out the flesh, following the natural grooves of the squash, making the grooves as deep as possible, and smoothing them with the back of a spoon.)

2 Melt the wax in the top part of the double boiler set over—not in—boiling water. As the wax melts, add the color tablets. If you want to make different-colored candles, melt the wax in batches.

3 Meanwhile, cut lengths of wick a few inches longer than the squash are tall. Attach the wick tabs to the wicks.

4 When the wax is completely melted, carefully pour into a squash. Drop in one wick tab, with the wick attached, and let it settle to the bottom. Lay a pencil across the top of the squash and drape the end of the wick over it so it is as centered as possible. Repeat, in batches if you like, to make more candles. Let the candles harden completely, 5 to 6 hours, then peel the squash away from the wax.

CHECKERBOARD PICTURE FRAME

MATERIALS

unpainted wooden picture frame

white, yellow, orange, and black acrylic paint

TOOLS

rags

orange colored pencil

ruler

sandpaper

small brush

Don't let a costumed child in the thrall of Halloween excitement escape the camera. Every year, take a photograph of your own children before they leave to go trick-or-treating as well as those who come to the door—the pictures will be treasured. And what better way to proudly display this year's costumes than in this lightly distressed wooden frame?

1 Remove the backing materials and glass from the frame. With a rag, rub the frame with the white paint. With a clean part of the rag, rub off most of the paint. Let dry. In the same way, rub in the yellow paint and rub off. Let dry.

2 With the orange pencil and a ruler, lightly sketch a checkerboard design on the frame. Paint in orange squares. Let dry. For a distressed look, lightly sand in some places and leave others as is. With the brush, paint the inner rim of the frame black. Assemble the frame with your picture, glass, and backing materials.

TRICK-OR-TREATERS PHOTO ALBUM

Craft a final resting place for Halloween photos and the kids' spookiest drawings.

MATERIALS

1 yard black felt

2 skeins white embroidery thread and needle

¾ yard paper-backed fusible web, such as HeatnBond Ultra Hold

scrap orange felt

two 11- by 14-inch pieces orange and black check fabric for lining

two 8½- by 11¾-inch pieces cardboard

4 eyelets

twelve 8½- by 11-inch pieces black construction paper for pages

50 inches black and white check ribbon

50 inches baby-size orange rickrack

TOOLS

ruler

scissors

marker

6- by 6-inch piece embroidery paper, such as Stitch and Treat

bone-scoring tool

fabric glue, such as Fabri-Tac

X-Acto knife

awl

hole punch

1 To make the covers: Cut out four 9- by 12-inch pieces of black felt. Write your title on the embroidery paper in stylized letters. Baste the paper to one piece of felt. Embroider with the thread. Remove the paper. Draw a hat, jack-o'-lantern, and broom on the backing of the fusible web and iron to the orange felt. Cut out, remove the backing, and iron to the same piece of black felt.

2 Baste the lettered piece of felt to a second piece and blanket stitch together. Repeat with the 2 remaining pieces of felt for the back.

3 Cut two 11- by 14-inch pieces of fusible web. Iron one to the wrong side of a piece of lining fabric. Remove the backing and carefully position the cardboard on the fabric. Press with an iron. Fold the edges over the back of the cardboard and iron. Repeat with the remaining piece of fabric.

4 On the nonfabric side of one piece of the cardboard, with the bone-scorer, score 1 inch from the edge on a long side (to allow the front cover to fold). Position and glue the front felt cover to the uncovered side of the scored cardboard. Repeat with the back felt cover and the other piece of cardboard.

5 One-half inch in from the edge and 2¾ inches from the top and bottom, make 2 small slits with the X-Acto knife into each cover. Use the awl to push through and make holes. Set in the eyelets.

6 Stack the pages and place between the covers. Mark the paper through the eyelets. Punch holes in the paper. Assemble the book. Thread the ribbon and rickrack through the holes and tie in front.

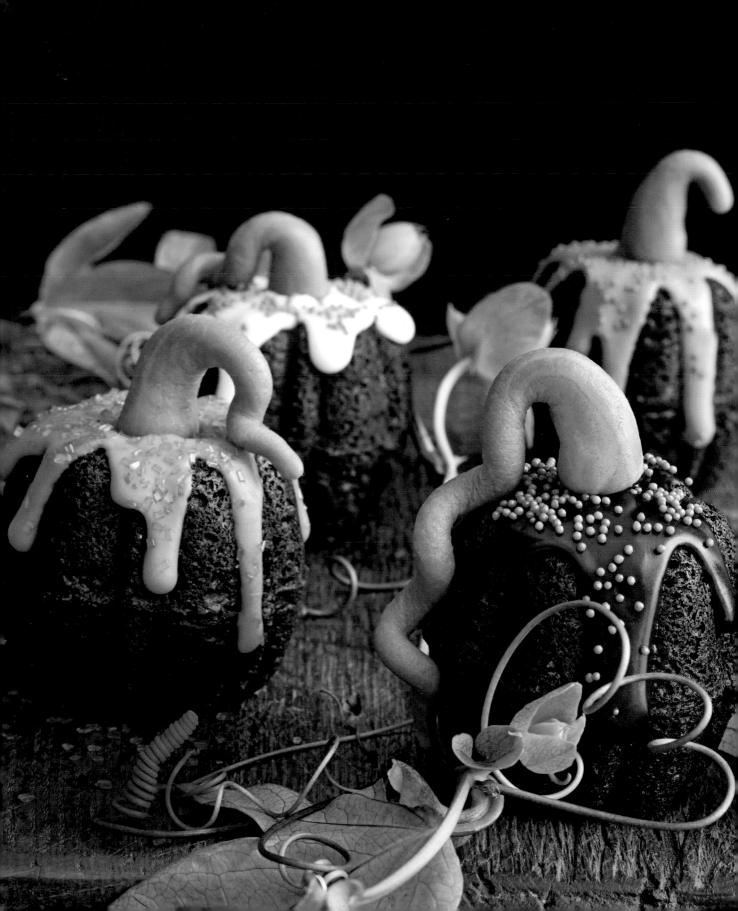

tantalizing recipes & bewitching parties

cast a spell with tempting treats

What is Halloween without delicious seasonal fare and lots of tempting sweets and treats? We've rounded up our favorite festive recipes so you'll have lots of options, whether you need eye-catching candies to keep trick-or-treaters happy or easy-to-execute dishes for a Halloween party or buffet.

We begin with a selection of beverages (including a few containing alcohol for the grown-ups), plus snacks and treats just right for party nibbles or to serve to impromptu guests. Since Halloween is all about cozy, casual entertaining, we've included ideas for simple starters and lots of buffet favorites to feed your family or an entire parade's worth of costumed kids and adults alike. And, of course, we haven't forgotten the baked goods, from cookies and brownies to show-stopping cakes, this section is filled with all sorts of delectable, celebratory treats.

Interspersed among the recipes, you'll find party plans, menus, and inspirations for three very special events: an outrageous kids' bash, a thoroughly grown-up fête, and a pumpkin-carving party that everyone will enjoy. You don't have to believe in ghosts and goblins to observe—and create anew—the traditions of the scariest night of the year.

The Recipes

beverages

SPARKLING SPICED CRANBERRY PUNCH

Light and refreshing; fit for a crowd.

MAKES 16 SERVINGS

2 cups water

½ cup sugar

4 3-inch cinnamon sticks

½ teaspoon whole cloves

ice cubes

2 8½-ounce packages liquid concentrated cranberry juice cocktail

2 1-liter bottles seltzer, chilled

1 In a 2-quart saucepan over high heat, heat the water, sugar, cinnamon sticks, and cloves to boiling. Remove from heat; let stand 15 minutes. Cover and refrigerate until cold.

2 Just before serving, strain the spice mixture over ice cubes into a small punch bowl. Add the cranberry juice concentrate and mix well. Stir in the seltzer and serve.

NUTRITION PER SERVING **Protein: 0G; Fat: 0G; Carbohydrate: 26G; Fiber: 0G; Sodium: 1.5MG; Cholesterol: 0MG; Calories: 102.**

HARVEST MOON COCKTAIL

These richly colored cocktails embody the spirit of the season.

lemon wedge

colored (orange or green) cocktail sugar

¼ cup apricot brandy

½ cup sweet-and-sour mix

½ cup seltzer water

4 teaspoons pomegranate juice

MAKES 2 SERVINGS

1 Dampen the rims of 2 martini glasses with a lemon wedge and dip them into the colored cocktail sugar.

2 Combine the brandy, sweet-and-sour mix, and seltzer in an ice-filled cocktail shaker, mix vigorously, and pour into the prepared glasses. Add 2 teaspoons of pomegranate juice to each glass (do not stir) and serve.

nutrition per serving **Protein: 12G; Fat: 0G; Carbohydrate: 18.7G; Fiber: 0G; Sodium: 64.7MG; Cholesterol: 0MG; Calories: 143.**

MULLED CIDER

- **8 cups (½ gallon) apple cider**
- **1 tablespoon whole allspice**
- **1 tablespoon whole cloves**
- **8 long cinnamon sticks**

Nothing could be simpler or more warming on a blustery night than apple cider, steaming and spiced. Before guests arrive, fill your home with a warm autumnal scent by heating this on the stove.

MAKES 8 SERVINGS

In a 3-quart saucepan, heat the cider, allspice, cloves, and cinnamon to boiling. With tongs, place a cinnamon stick in each of 8 mugs. Strain hot cider into the mugs and serve.

NUTRITION PER SERVING   **Protein: 0G; Fat: 0G; Carbohydrate: 30G; Fiber: 0G; Sodium: 25MG; Cholesterol: 0MG; Calories: 120.**

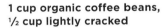

1 cup organic coffee beans,
½ cup lightly cracked

3 cups whole milk

1½ 3-inch cinnamon sticks,
broken

4 whole green cardamom
pods

¼ cup honey

1 ounce rum, such as Mount
Gay (optional)

WHITE SPICED COFFEE

A perfect substitute for, or companion to, dessert.

MAKES 3 SERVINGS –

1 Place the coffee beans and spices in a sealable plastic bag and use a heavy-bottomed skillet to crack them. Place the milk and crushed coffee beans in a saucepan. Heat the mixture to a simmer over medium-high heat—about 7 minutes. Immediately remove from the heat and let the beans steep in the milk for 15 minutes.

2 Strain the coffee mixture into the jar of a blender. Discard the crushed coffee beans. Add the cinnamon sticks, cardamom, and honey to the steeped milk and blend on high speed until the spices are coarsely ground—about 30 seconds.

3 Strain the liquid back into the saucepan and discard the ground spices. Rewarm the spiced coffee over medium-high heat until the liquid is hot and steaming. Add rum, if desired. Pour into warmed coffee mugs, and serve hot.

– –
NUTRITION PER SERVING   **Protein: 9.5G; Fat: 22.7G; Carbohydrate: 43.5G; Fiber: 0.5G; Sodium: 116MG; Cholesterol: 79MG; Calories: 404.**
– –

snacks & treats

SUGAR-AND-SPICE ALMONDS

Place these nibbles in small bowls around the house at Halloween—adults and kids alike will gobble them up.

⅓ cup sugar

4 teaspoons ground cinnamon

½ teaspoon ground nutmeg

2 cups natural whole almonds

3 tablespoons light corn syrup

MAKES 2 CUPS

1 Preheat the oven to 350°F. Coat a rimmed baking sheet with nonstick cooking spray.

2 In a cup or small bowl, combine the sugar, cinnamon, and nutmeg; set aside. In a medium-size bowl, stir together the almonds and corn syrup until the almonds are well coated.

3 Add the sugar mixture to the almond mixture, stirring until well combined. Spread on the prepared baking sheet and bake about 10 minutes, or until the sugar coating is bubbly and the almonds are browned.

4 Let cool on the baking sheet to room temperature, stirring occasionally to prevent sticking and to separate the almonds. Store in an airtight container.

nutrition per 2 tablespoons **Protein: 3.8G; Fat: 8.9G; Carbohydrate: 11.8G; Fiber: 2.5G; Sodium: 2.8MG; Cholesterol: 0MG; Calories: 133.**

ROASTED PUMPKIN SEEDS

1 cup raw pumpkin seeds, separated from fibers

1 teaspoon olive or corn oil

¼ teaspoon salt

Don't throw out those seeds when carving a jack-o'-lantern: They make a wonderful, crunchy snack. If you have more than one cup of seeds, simply multiply the oil and salt accordingly.

MAKES 1 CUP

1 Preheat the oven to 350°F. Rub the pumpkin seeds in a cloth towel to separate them from any remaining fibers.

2 On a rimmed baking sheet, combine the seeds, oil, and salt. Spread out in a single layer. Bake 10 to 15 minutes, or until the seeds are dry and just beginning to brown. Let cool and serve.

NUTRITION PER ¼ CUP   Protein: 10.7G; Fat: 22.4G; Carbohydrate: 5.3G; Fiber: 1.3G; Sodium: 152MG; Cholesterol: 0MG; Calories: 263.

SPICED PECANS

1 teaspoon olive oil

2 cups pecan halves

¼ cup firmly packed light brown sugar

¼ cup melted butter

4 teaspoons Mexican hot sauce, such as Cholula

1 teaspoon salt

½ teaspoon ground black pepper

A delectable party snack, these sweet-hot nuts are also a perfect salad topper. See Red Pear, Grape, and Pecan Salad (recipe, page 125).

MAKES 2 CUPS

1 Preheat the oven to 350°F. Brush olive oil on a baking sheet. Toss the pecan halves, sugar, butter, hot sauce, salt, and pepper together in medium bowl and spread evenly into one layer on baking sheet.

2 Bake, stirring once, until lightly toasted—about 20 minutes. Cool and serve in a bowl or as a salad topper.

NUTRITION PER 2 TABLESPOONS   Protein: 2G; Fat: 12G; Carbohydrate: 4G; Fiber: 2G; Sodium: 180MG; Cholesterol: 10MG; Calories: 120.

CAKE DOUGHNUTS

3 cups unsifted all-purpose flour

1 cup sugar

1 tablespoon baking powder

1½ teaspoons cinnamon

½ teaspoon salt

¼ teaspoon ground nutmeg

1 cup milk

1 large egg

¼ cup melted butter or margarine

vegetable oil, for frying

Offer both sugar and cinnamon versions of these tender doughnuts to your guests. For more fun options, see Quick and Easy Doughnut Toppings, opposite.

MAKES ABOUT 16 DOUGHNUTS AND 16 HOLES

1 In a large bowl, combine the flour, ½ cup sugar, the baking powder, 1 teaspoon cinnamon, the salt, and nutmeg. In a small bowl, combine the milk, egg, and butter. Stir the milk mixture into the flour mixture until well combined. Cover and refrigerate the dough at least 1 hour.

2 On a well-floured board, with a floured rolling pin, roll out the dough to a ½-inch thickness. Using a lightly floured 3-inch doughnut cutter with center in place, cut out doughnuts and holes. Pat the scraps together to form more 3-inch rounds (do not reroll them) and cut with the doughnut cutter.

3 In a 3-quart saucepan, heat 2 inches vegetable oil to 370°F. Fry the doughnuts and holes, a few at a time, turning often, 2 to 3 minutes, or until golden brown. Drain on paper towels.

4 In a small plastic or paper bag, combine ¼ cup sugar and the remaining ½ teaspoon cinnamon. Put the remaining ¼ cup sugar into another bag. Toss half the doughnuts and holes, a few at a time, in the bag to coat with the cinnamon-sugar mixture. Toss the remaining doughnuts and holes in the plain sugar.

NUTRITION PER DOUGHNUT   Protein: 2.7G; Fat: 6.6G; Carbohydrate: 25.5G; Fiber: .6G; Sodium: 165.8MG; Cholesterol: 17.9MG; Calories: 171.

NUTRITION PER DOUGHNUT HOLE   Protein: .5G; Fat: 1.3G; Carbohydrate: 5.1G; Fiber: .1G; Sodium: 53.2MG; Cholesterol: 3.6MG; Calories: 34.

Quick & Easy Doughnut Toppings

It's hard to imagine a more irresistible snack than a doughnut. But we did! Chocolate cake doughnuts, cider doughnuts, and old-fashioned styles from a bakery or a supermarket are sturdy enough to withstand spreads and toppings, or bake the Cake Doughnuts in the recipe opposite. Then top with Cream-Cheese Pumpkin Icing and sprinkle with one of the toppings suggested below. Wondering if day-olds are okay? Absolutely! Heat them in a toaster oven to bring out their cakelike flavor.

{ VARIATIONS }

Cream-Cheese Pumpkin Icing: Beat 4 ounces cream cheese, and 2 tablespoons each softened butter and pumpkin puree, with 2 cups confectioners' sugar, ⅛ teaspoon ground cinnamon, and ½ teaspoon vanilla until light and creamy. Keep chilled until ready to use. Makes 1 ¾ cups.

If it's in a little bottle with a shaker at the top, it can probably be sprinkled on a doughnut. We like **pumpkin-pie spice** on the cream-cheese icing, or a tiny bit of cinnamon over honey and peanut butter. For a treat that's perfect for parties and kids, sprinkle with colorful toppings, such as those below.

* **Decoratifs:** Tiny spheres that suggest pumpkins add a playful note.
* **Nonpareils:** Hint at Halloween with a sprinkling of this fun topping.
* **Sparkling Sugar:** Brighten treats with the fall-friendly color.

MAPLE POPCORN

Serve this traditional American treat shortly after it is made, while it is at its crisp best.

⅓ cup unpopped popcorn

⅔ cup sugar

⅔ cup water

⅛ teaspoon cream of tartar

⅔ cup maple syrup

2 tablespoons butter

½ teaspoon salt

MAKES ABOUT 2 QUARTS

1 Pop the popcorn in a hot air popper into a large bowl. Generously grease a baking sheet.

2 In a heavy 1½-quart saucepan fitted with a candy thermometer (see Candy-making Tricks, below), bring the sugar, water, and cream of tartar to a boil over high heat, stirring occasionally. Brush the side of the pan with warm water to dissolve any crystals forming at the edge. Reduce the heat to medium and continue cooking, without stirring, about 10 minutes, until the mixture is a deep golden brown and the temperature reaches 260°F.

3 Carefully stir in the maple syrup and cook 2 minutes longer. Remove from heat. Stir in the butter and salt until the butter melts. Immediately pour the sugar mixture over the popcorn: With a long-handled spoon, carefully stir the popcorn to coat thoroughly with the sugar mixture (do not use your hands; the syrup is very hot). Pour onto greased baking sheet to cool before serving.

NUTRITION PER CUP **Protein: 1G; Fat: 3.3G; Carbohydrate: 41.6G; Fiber: 1.2G; Sodium: 168.9MG; Cholesterol: 7.6MG; Calories: 195.**

Candy-making Tricks

Getting sugar to the right temperature and consistency is the most important step in candy making. To properly gauge the temperature, use a candy thermometer that can be clipped to the side of the pan. For an accurate reading, avoid touching the probe to the bottom of the pan, and check the temperature in several spots.

DRIED FRUIT AND POPCORN BALLS

For a festive presentation, wrap room-temperature popcorn balls in orange- and black-colored cellophane and tie them closed with coordinating ribbon.

12 cups popped popcorn

3 cups mixed dried fruit (such as golden raisins, cherries, chopped apricots and figs)

1¼ cups granulated sugar

¾ cup firmly packed brown sugar

1 cup corn syrup

½ cup water

MAKES 12 POPCORN BALLS

1 Toss the popcorn with the dried fruit in a large, lightly oiled, heatproof bowl. Oil 2 waxed paper–lined baking pans and a long metal fork. Set aside.

2 In a heavy 2-quart saucepan fitted with a candy thermometer (see Candy-making Tricks, opposite), bring the sugar, brown sugar, corn syrup, and water to a boil over medium-high heat, stirring occasionally. Reduce the heat to medium and continue cooking, without stirring, about 10 minutes, until the mixture is deep golden brown and the temperature reaches 260°F.

3 Carefully pour the syrup over the popcorn mixture. Stir with a fork to distribute. Let sit for 1 to 2 minutes. With well-oiled hands, form 3-inch balls, place on pans, and cool completely. Store in an airtight container for up to 4 days. To avoid a sticky mess, serve on plates or in shallow bowls.

nutrition per popcorn ball **Protein: 2.1G; Fat: 1.5G; Carbohydrate: 91.3G; Fiber: 3.2G; Sodium: 77.7MG; Cholesterol: 0MG; Calories: 378.**

{VARIATIONS}

For truly festive popcorn balls, omit the chunks of dried fruit and **substitute black and orange jelly beans** and roasted pumpkin seeds. To please chocolate lovers, drizzle the finished popcorn balls with **melted dark chocolate** and let set on waxed paper.

CARAMEL ACORN CANDIES

These whimsical acorn-shaped caramels are delicious and can jazz up your Halloween décor, too. Scatter them around the serving dishes on the buffet table or use to fill small bowls around the room. Melted chocolate chips make the caps for the acorns.

1 14-ounce can sweetened condensed milk (not evaporated milk)

1 cup light corn syrup

1/8 teaspoon salt

1 teaspoon vanilla extract

1/2 cup semisweet chocolate chips

1/2 cup finely chopped walnuts

MAKES ABOUT 5 DOZEN

1 Line the bottom and 2 sides of an 8-inch-square baking pan with aluminum foil. Butter the foil on the bottom of the pan; set aside.

2 In a heavy 1 1/2-quart saucepan fitted with a candy thermometer (see Candy-making Tricks, page 112), heat the condensed milk, corn syrup, and salt over medium heat to boiling, stirring constantly. Continue to cook and stir over medium-low heat for 15 to 20 minutes, until the mixture thickens and the temperature reaches 238°F, or the soft-ball stage. Remove from heat and stir in the vanilla. Pour into the prepared pan, spreading evenly. Cool in the pan on a wire rack just until firm enough to cut.

3 Lift the candy from the pan and peel off the foil. Cut the candy into 1-inch pieces. Shape each into an acorn, with one end slightly wider and flatter than the other. Place on a tray and refrigerate until firm.

4 Place the chocolate chips in a cup and set in a small saucepan with 1 inch of hot water. Place the pan over medium heat and melt the chocolate until smooth. Remove the cup from the pan. Dip the flat end of each caramel acorn into the chocolate, then into the walnuts. Let the chocolate set. Store the candies in a single layer in a container in the refrigerator.

nutrition per candy **Protein: .7G; Fat: 1.6G; Carbohydrate: 9.1G; Fiber: .2G; Sodium: 17.1MG; Cholesterol: 2.3MG; Calories: 51.**

CARAMEL APPLES

12 crisp apples

1⅓ cups dark corn syrup

1⅓ cups granulated sugar

1⅓ cups firmly packed
light brown sugar

1⅓ cups heavy cream

¼ teaspoon salt

3 tablespoons butter

¾ teaspoon vanilla extract

Want to dress up your apples for the party? Wrap colored ribbon or raffia around wooden candy apple sticks and tie them in a bow. Use two colors to create a striped effect. Secure with glue at the blunt end that won't be inserted into the apple.

MAKES 12 APPLES

1 Line a baking pan with a generously oiled sheet of parchment paper. Push a candy apple stick into the core of each apple.

2 In a heavy 2-quart saucepan fitted with a candy thermometer (see Candy-making Tricks, page 112), combine the syrup, sugars, heavy cream, and salt in a large saucepan over medium-high heat. Simmer until the mixture reaches 270°F—about 15 minutes. Remove from heat, stir in the butter and vanilla. Let cool for 6 to 8 minutes, until caramel thickens to a toffeelike consistency.

3 Dip and gently swirl the apples into the caramel and place on the prepared baking sheet. Let cool completely.

NUTRITION PER APPLE **Protein: 1G; Fat: 15G; Carbohydrate: 148G; Fiber: 3G; Sodium: 220MG; Cholesterol: 55MG; Calories: 700.**

{VARIATIONS}

Fancy Caramel Apples: Dip apples in melted nonpareils. Or roll caramel-covered apples in pumpkin seeds or chopped roasted nuts, or drizzle with melted chocolate (see photo, page 176).

Caramel Bonus!

Make candies from the caramel left over after apple dipping. While the caramel is still warm, pour it into an 8-inch square, oiled baking dish. Cool until caramel is a solid but pliable slab. Remove from the dish, place the slab on a cutting board, and slice into 1-inch pieces using a chef's knife. Wrap each piece in a square of waxed paper, twisting the ends to seal. Store in an airtight container for up to 2 weeks.

kids' halloween bash

Prepare to scare! Host a haunted Halloween celebration the kids will love. Whether your party is a substitute for trick-or-treating or a follow-up to the candy frenzy, it's frighteningly easy to scare up a good time. Set the tone with invitations in the shape of tombstones "engraved" with the guests' names. Or enlist your kids to help you whip up some easy Slash-and-Paste "Boo" or Pumpkin Invitations (see pages 74-75). Be sure to welcome revelers with a decked out walkway and front door: Skeleton Luminarias and the Front-Door Scarecrow (see pages 64 and 68, respectively) will let everyone know the party is at your place.

Cute party favors are essential: How about pencils embellished with pumpkins made from small Styrofoam balls painted orange; miniature pumpkins that the kids can decorate with pens or paints as part of the party; or paper-bag pumpkins, made by stuffing a brown paper bag with newspaper, twisting the top to create a stem, and painting on a jack-o'-lantern face? Your guests would also dig Candy Corn Placeholders or the Trick-or-Treat Surprises tied with black licorice and topped with creepy plastic spiders (see pages 80 and 191, respectively).

For creepy decorating ideas, see Chapter 2: Enchanting Handmade Decorations, page 57. Of course, you can't forget the all-important jack-o'-lantern. Why not carve a mixed assortment to deck out your yard and home? Chapter 1: Spooky Jack-o'-Lanterns and Artful Pumpkins, page 11, contains dozens of playful pumpkin-carving ideas sure to delight your guests.

Halloween Treats and Sweets

If a roomful of little ghouls are staying for dinner, here's **a fun menu** that will appeal to even the pickiest eaters.

Apple Juice

Dried Fruit and Popcorn Balls, page 113

Carrot-Raisin Salad with Toasted Walnuts, page 124

Mini Corn Dogs, page 136

Baked Macaroni with Three Cheeses, page 137

Molasses Cookies, page 148

Spooky Black Cat Cake, page 171

ABOVE, FROM LEFT TO RIGHT: **One jack-o'-lantern will do the job, but why not delight your guests with a humorous display of multiple carved pumpkins? Molasses cookies with a creamy frosting, center, are sure to please. Serve Baked Macaroni and Three Cheeses, right, to ensure that the kids eat something besides sweets at the party.** OPPOSITE PAGE: **What child wouldn't adore this sparkly Spooky Cat Cake? To create the stencil, simply photocopy the cover of this book and cut out the cat shape.**

Children like to be scared, but not too scared. Start them off gently, with a project that requires concentration and creativity. Brown-paper bags (painted black or white ahead of time if you wish), or white paper plates (with string attached for tying around a small head), are quick and easy masks. Cut two holes for eyes, and set up an assortment of poster paints, crayons, or markers—whatever is best for the age group—to let the children express themselves. Then let the Halloween games begin!

✳ Weather permitting, organize an outdoor pumpkin hunt. Hide miniature pumpkins and have the children search until each one has found a pumpkin. If the children are older, a scavenger hunt is more challenging.

Yucky Yummies

Black, orange, and/or yucky is the **finger food** of choice at a children's Halloween party. Here are some **blood-curdling recipes** you can serve in your buffet.

✳ As far as kids are concerned, the grosser the better: Be sure to serve a tray of "dirt" and "worms" fresh from the graveyard. Bake crumbly brownies or dark chocolate cookies. Break into bite-sized pieces, mix with gummy worms, and garnish with lots of crumbs!

✳ Not gross enough? Serve up some Severed Fingers: Wrap hot dogs in a thin layer of biscuit dough. Bake and serve with a slivered almond "fingernail" at one end and a drop of "bloody" ketchup at the other.

✳ Grosser still: Hollow out good-sized oranges by cutting off the tops and scooping out the insides with a serrated-edge grapefruit spoon. With a felt-tipped pen, draw a jack-o'-lantern face on each orange. Fill with squares of red Jell-O, bits of the orange segments, and cantaloupe chunks. Tell the little party guests that each head is filled with brains.

✳ For thirsty revelers, whip up Dracula's favorite, a "blood" milkshake: In a blender, combine vanilla yogurt, frozen strawberries or raspberries, and a few ice cubes. Or blend cranberry and orange juice with a dollop of raspberry sherbet.

✳ For creepier slurps, make vampire-eyeball ice cubes. The day before the party, fill ice cube trays halfway with cranberry juice. Freeze until the juice is slush, then stick a green grape in the middle and put back in the freezer. Pop one in each drink.

* Fill a room with orange and black balloons. The goal is to cross the room without breaking any of the balloons—the challenge is that each participant is blindfolded!

* Wrap-the-Mummy may sound like mayhem, but it is guranteed to top a child's list of favorite party activities. Pair children off so that one is the mummy and the other is the mummy wrapper. Each pair gets a roll of white bath tissue with instructions to "wrap the mummy!" After one mummy is wrapped, it's then the turn of the partner to "wrap the mummy."

* Making a tape of Halloween noises is fun, and the tape can then be used in your haunted house (see page 122). Each child can make a noise into the tape recorder. Suggest shrieking, moaning and groaning, thunder (rattle a sheet of poster board), fire (crinkle a cellophane bag), evil laughing, chains clanging, wind howling, footsteps clomping, an owl hooting, a wolf howling, a witch cackling, a door opening, a ghost laughing, a cat meowing.

* Make Halloween finger puppets and invite the children (or older siblings) to make up stories.

* Create a list of all the words associated with Halloween (the children can shout them out) and then write poems using the words.

* Organize a "Monster Mash" dance contest—to the classic tune of course!

* Set up a Mad Scientist's Lab. Gross out your guests with bowls of "eyeballs" (peeled grapes), "guts" (cold spaghetti), "liver" (red or purple Jell-O), and "brains" (cooked cauliflower).

* Add a Halloween twist to classic party games: "Mother May I?" becomes "Mummy May I?"; "Pin the Tail on the Donkey" becomes "Pin the Spider on the Spiderweb"; "Simon Says" becomes "Dracula Says."

The Spookiest Haunted House

Whether you're creating an intimate little haunted house for ghostly guests or opening your doors to all the neighborhood trick-or-treaters, these tips will help you design a **spook-tacular experience**. It's scarier if you escort the guests through the haunted rooms in small groups. As the kids leave, **reward their bravery** with a sweet treat: a handful of candy from a black cauldron full of goodies.

❋ First impressions set the stage: In the yard or up a walkway, stick picnic torches spray-painted black in the ground and place a lighted candle in each.

❋ Make a **graveyard** in the front yard by cutting tombstones out of foamboard bought at an art supply store. Spray-paint the foamboard gray and add dabs of green paint for age. Think up funny names like "Al B. Seenyu," "Ima Ghost," and "R.U. Scared," and paint them in black.

❋ Cut large silhouettes of **menacing figures or ghosts** out of black poster board. Hang in windows with string or tape. Light from behind for best effect.

❋ Hang black fabric at the entrance to the haunted rooms.

❋ Tilt pictures on walls at odd angles (look for "instant ancestor" portraits in junk stores or at yard sales, the more severe and scary, the better!).

❋ Play a homemade tape of **creepy noises**: see page 121 for ideas.

❋ Take dead tree branches and stretch spiderwebbing (available from Halloween and party supply stores) from branch to branch; place rubber spiders and large bats cut from black construction paper in the webbing. For more atmosphere, drape sphagnum moss (from florist supply shops) from branches.

❋ Scatter dead, wilted flower arrangements around the house.

❋ Replace bulbs in lamps with flicker bulbs, and use artists' clip-on lamps covered with colored gels (red, green, and blue all give off an eerie light) to **cast scary shadows**.

❋ Weave **a massive spiderweb** in a doorway by taping rope across the top and tying dozens of pieces of long thread to it. Let the thread hang down to a couple of feet above the floor. As children pass through the doorway, the threads will feel like creepy spiderwebs.

* Use a projector to project **spooky slides or shadows** onto the ceiling or walls of a darkened room.

* For a **wizard's study**, place around the room, on shelves, or above doors old bottles filled with colored water, old books, old clocks, a crystal ball, or old rusty tools such as hatches and saw blades (these should be out of the reach of children). Pull spiderwebbing very thinly around the props.

* Clear most of the furniture from a room and cover the remaining pieces with the inexpensive black fabric used for lining clothing. Shred with a single-edged razor and cut hems unevenly to give the **appearance of age**.

easy starters & sides

CARROT-RAISIN SALAD WITH TOASTED WALNUTS

You won't have any trouble getting the kids to eat this salad—it's all dressed up in the spooky colors of the day! Serve cold or at room temperature. Double the recipe if you are expecting a lot of guests.

MAKES 6 SERVINGS

¾ cup orange juice

½ cup walnut or vegetable oil

1 tablespoon honey

¼ teaspoon salt

1½ pounds carrots, peeled and coarsely shredded

¾ cup dark seedless raisins

⅔ cup walnuts, coarsely chopped and toasted (See Nut-toasting Know-how, page 131)

In a medium bowl, with a wire whisk, beat together the orange juice, oil, honey, and salt. Stir the carrots, raisins, and walnuts into the dressing. Refrigerate covered, several hours or overnight. Toss just before serving.

NUTRITION PER SERVING **Protein: 3.5G; Fat: 16.7G; Carbohydrate: 33.6G; Fiber: 4.4G; Sodium: 169.5MG; Cholesterol: 0MG; Calories: 280.**

RED PEAR, GRAPE, AND PECAN SALAD

Simplify entertaining by making the salad and spicy pecans ahead; but dress just before serving.

- ³/₄ cup balsamic vinegar

- ½ cup olive oil

- 6 tablespoons firmly packed light brown sugar

- ½ teaspoon salt

- ¼ teaspoon ground black pepper

- 1 head red leaf or butter lettuce

- 1 pomegranate, seeded

- 32 large, dark seedless grapes, halved

- 1 large red onion, sliced into thin rings

- ½ cup crumbled blue cheese

- 4 ripe red pears, cored and sliced ½ inch thick

- 1 cup Spiced Pecans (recipe, page 133)

- zest of 2 oranges

MAKES 8 SERVINGS -

1 Combine vinegar, oil, brown sugar, salt, and pepper in a small saucepan over medium heat and stir until sugar is dissolved.

2 Tear lettuce into bite-size pieces. Wash and drain in a salad spinner. Divide evenly on 8 plates. Evenly divide and sprinkle pomegranate seeds, grape halves, red onion, cheese, pears, and pecans on each plate.

3 Drizzle vinaigrette on each salad and sprinkle with orange zest. Serve immediately.

- -

NUTRITION PER SERVING   Protein: 5G; Fat: 30G; Carbohydrate: 43G; Fiber: 5G; Sodium: 480MG; Cholesterol: 15MG; Calories: 440.

- -

MARINATED VEGETABLE SALAD

1 large (2 ½ pounds) head cauliflower

1 pound carrots, peeled

½ cup extra-virgin olive oil

¼ cup red-wine vinegar

⅓ cup fresh parsley leaves, chopped

1 teaspoon sugar

¾ teaspoon salt

½ teaspoon dry mustard

¼ teaspoon ground black pepper

1 cup brine-cured green and ripe olives

Fresh flat-leaf or Italian parsley sprigs (optional)

Green and ripe olives mingle with cauliflower and carrots in this marinated salad. This recipe, which improves in flavor when refrigerated overnight, is an ideal make-ahead party dish.

MAKES 12 SERVINGS

1 Trim the cauliflower and separate or cut it into small flowerets. Cut the carrots into 2½- to 3-inch by ½-inch sticks. In a 5-quart saucepan, heat 2 inches water to boiling over high heat. Add the carrots and reheat the water to boiling.

2 Add the cauliflower to the carrots. Cook the vegetables just until tender-crisp—7 to 10 minutes. Drain the vegetables and rinse with cold water; set aside in a large bowl or food-storage container.

3 In a jar with a tight-fitting lid, combine the oil, vinegar, chopped parsley, sugar, salt, dry mustard, and pepper until well mixed. Pour the marinade over the vegetables; toss and cover. Refrigerate for 2 hours or overnight, stirring occasionally.

4 Just before serving, add the olives to the vegetables and toss until well mixed. Transfer to a serving bowl. Garnish with parsley sprigs, if desired.

nutrition per serving **Protein: 2G; Fat: 11G; Carbohydrate: 9G; Fiber: 4G; Sodium: 380MG; Cholesterol: 0MG; Calories: 200.**

WILD MUSHROOM TOASTS

A sophisticated starter for a grown-up All Hallow's Eve celebration.

3 pounds mixed fresh mushrooms; plus 3 ounces dried mushrooms

¼ cup olive oil

3 tablespoons finely chopped shallots

6 cloves garlic, crushed

½ cup chicken broth

2 tablespoons cognac

2 tablespoons butter

1½ teaspoons salt

½ teaspoon ground black pepper

2 sprigs each rosemary and thyme

¼ cup chopped flat-leaf parsley

1 loaf garlic bread

1¼ ounces shaved Parmesan (about ⅓ cup)

MAKES 6 SERVINGS

1 Preheat the oven to 450F°. Clean, stem, and slice the fresh mushrooms ¼ inch thick. Soak the dried mushrooms in a bowl of hot water until tender—about 10 minutes. Rinse and squeeze to dry.

2 Heat a 12-inch ovenproof skillet until very hot. Add the olive oil and fresh mushrooms. Cook, while stirring frequently, over high heat until mushrooms release their liquid—about 10 minutes. Add the shallots, garlic, and rehydrated mushrooms. Cook until the liquid has evaporated. Add the broth, cognac, butter, salt, pepper, and rosemary and thyme sprigs.

3 Transfer skillet to the oven and roast, stirring twice, for 30 minutes. Stir in the parsley. Serve warm on the garlic bread with Parmesan curls.

NUTRITION PER SERVING **Protein: 13G; Fat: 15G; Carbohydrate: 17G; Fiber: 6G; Sodium: 700MG; Cholesterol: 15MG; Calories: 260.**

INDIAN SHUCK BREAD

- 12 dried corn husks
- 2 cups yellow cornmeal
- 1 tablespoon firmly packed light brown sugar
- 1 teaspoon ground cinnamon
- 1 teaspoon baking powder
- ½ teaspoon salt
- ¼ teaspoon cayenne pepper
- 1½ cups boiling water

Impress your guests by presenting these intriguing little corn-husk bundles at table. Chill the Maple Butter in decorative molds, such as the maple-leaf shape shown in photo.

MAKES 12 SERVINGS

1 Soak the corn husks in water until softened—1 hour. Blot dry and tear off 24 quarter-inch strips from the husks and set them and the larger husks aside.

2 Stir together the cornmeal, brown sugar, cinnamon, baking powder, salt, and cayenne with the boiling water until a soft dough forms. Pat the dough into 1- by 3-inch logs using about 2½ tablespoons dough per log. Wrap each log with the larger corn husk pieces and tie the ends with the reserved strips to form a packet.

3 Fill a large saucepan halfway with water and bring to a boil. Add the packets and cook for 15 minutes. Remove and serve while still hot, in the husks, along with the Maple Butter.

NUTRITION PER SERVING **Protein: 2G; Fat: .5G; Carbohydrate: 17G; Fiber: 2G; Sodium: 150MG; Cholesterol: 0MG; Calories: 80.**

MAPLE BUTTER

- 1 cup (2 sticks) butter, softened
- ¼ cup maple syrup
- ½ teaspoon Mexican hot sauce, such as Cholula (optional)

Beat the butter, syrup, and hot sauce together until combined. Transfer to a parchment paper–lined baking pan and cover with another sheet of parchment paper. Press, using a rolling pin, to pack the butter to form a ½-inch-thick slab. Chill for 30 minutes. Remove top sheet of parchment paper and cut butter into pats.

NUTRITION PER TABLESPOON **Protein: 0G; Fat: 11G; Carbohydrate: 3G; Fiber: 0G; Sodium: 5MG; Cholesterol: 30MG; Calories: 110.**

GREEN BEANS WITH SMOKED BACON AND ONIONS

A perfect addition to any buffet table or potluck.

MAKES 8 SERVINGS

2 pounds green beans, trimmed

2¼ teaspoons salt

4 slices thick-cut smoked bacon, cut into 1-inch-wide strips

1 medium onion, cut into 1-inch pieces

1 Prepare an ice bath. Bring a large saucepan of water to a boil. Add the beans and 2 teaspoons salt, and cook just until the beans turn bright green—about 7 minutes. Drain the beans and plunge them into the ice bath until they're cool. Remove beans from the bath, and drain on a towel.

2 Add the bacon to a large skillet over medium-high heat and cook until golden brown and lightly crisp. Drain all but 2 tablespoons of the bacon fat.

3 Add the blanched beans, onion pieces, and remaining salt and toss to completely coat with the fat. Reduce heat to medium, and cook until the beans are warmed through and the onions have softened—4 to 5 minutes. Serve immediately.

nutrition per serving **Protein: 3.2G; Fat: 2.2G; Carbohydrate: 8.9G; Fiber: 4G; Sodium: 465MG; Cholesterol: 5MG; Calories: 58.**

MAPLE-PECAN SWEET POTATOES

Golden chunks of sweet potato coated in a beautiful amber glaze.

8 medium-size sweet potatoes (about 3½ pounds), peeled and cut into 1½-inch chunks

½ cup firmly packed light brown sugar

⅓ cup maple syrup

¼ cup (½ stick) butter or margarine

¼ teaspoon salt

⅛ teaspoon ground black pepper

¼ cup pecan halves, toasted (see Nut-toasting Know-how, below)

MAKES 8 SERVINGS

1 Cook the sweet potatoes in a large saucepan of boiling water about 20 minutes, or until tender. Drain well.

2 Meanwhile, in a 1-quart saucepan, combine the brown sugar, maple syrup, butter, salt, and pepper. Heat to boiling over medium-high heat. Reduce the heat to low. Cook, stirring constantly, about 2 minutes, or until clear and thickened.

3 Transfer the potatoes to a serving dish, top with the syrup mixture, sprinkle with the pecans, and serve.

nutrition per serving Protein: 2.5G; Fat: 8.4G; Carbohydrate: 50.3G; Fiber: 4.2G; Sodium: 160.4MG; Cholesterol: 15.3MG; Calories: 279.

Nut-toasting Know-how

Toasting nuts is a great way to bring out their flavor. Here's a simple method for toasting pecans, walnuts, or almonds. Preheat the oven to 350°F. Arrange the shelled nuts in a single layer on a baking sheet. Toast about 10 minutes, stirring occasionally, until the nuts are lightly browned and fragrant. Watch closely, though, as nuts are easy to burn! Let the nuts cool before chopping.

ACORN SQUASH STUFFED WITH RUTABAGA AND PECANS

Festive and oh so good.

2 medium acorn squashes, halved and inside pulp scraped out

1 tablespoon vegetable oil

1 large rutabaga

1 teaspoon salt

½ cup toasted pecans (see Nut-toasting Know-how, page 131)

½ cup (1 stick) butter

¼ cup firmly packed light brown sugar

¼ cup honey

⅛ teaspoon allspice

MAKES 8 SERVINGS

1 Roast the squash: Preheat the oven to 350°F. Use a sharp knife to trim the bottom of each squash half to form a flat surface. Rub with vegetable oil. Place the squash halves cut sides down in an ovenproof baking dish. Bake until the squash are tender when pierced with a sharp knife—about 35 minutes.

2 Stuff the squash: Peel and cut the rutabaga into 1-inch pieces and place in a large skillet. Cover with cold water, add the salt, and bring to a boil over high heat. Cover the skillet with a tight-fitting lid and cook until the vegetables are tender when pierced with the tip of a sharp knife—8 to 10 minutes. Coarsely chop ¼ cup of the pecans in a food processor fitted with a steel blade. Add the butter and brown sugar and pulse to blend. Turn the squash over so the rind sides are down and fill the centers with the cooked rutabaga. Spoon an equal amount of the pecan butter into each of the centers.

3 Increase oven temperature to 400°F. Drizzle the squash with the honey and dust with the allspice and remaining pecans. Roast for an additional 15 minutes. Slice the squash halves into quarters, if desired, and serve immediately.

nutrition per serving Protein: 1.9G; Fat: 18.1G; Carbohydrate: 25.2G; Fiber: 3.1G; Sodium: 282MG; Cholesterol: 31MG; Calories: 257.

SWEET POTATO BISCUITS

You'll be amazed to see how quickly your friends and family gobble up a basket of these rolls. Warm or room-temperature, they are tender and delicious.

MAKES ABOUT 18 BISCUITS

- 2 ½ cups all-purpose flour
- 2 tablespoons baking powder
- ⅛ teaspoon allspice
- ⅛ teaspoon ground cloves
- ½ teaspoon salt
- ¼ cup firmly packed light brown sugar
- ½ cup (1 stick) butter, chilled
- ¼ cup shortening, chilled
- 1 ½ cups sweet potatoes, cooked and mashed
- 2 tablespoons milk

1 Preheat the oven to 425°F. Sift the flour, baking powder, allspice, cloves, and salt in a large bowl. Use the tips of your fingers to blend in the brown sugar. Cut in the chilled butter and shortening with a pastry cutter or by pulsing in a food processor, until the mixture resembles coarse, crumbly meal. Then stir in the mashed sweet potatoes, and knead until the dough just holds together.

2 Turn the dough onto a lightly floured surface. Knead gently for 1 minute, adding a little flour as necessary to incorporate all the ingredients. Pat the dough in a ½-inch circle and let it rest, covered with a clean towel, for 10 to 15 minutes.

3 Cut out the biscuits with a 2-inch round cutter dipped in flour. Gather the scraps, pat out again, and cut into biscuits.

4 Arrange them about ¾ inch apart on an ungreased baking sheet and brush the tops with milk. Bake until golden brown—10 to 15 minutes. Cool the biscuits on a rack. Serve warm or room temperature.

nutrition per serving **Protein: 2.3G; Fat: 5.7G; Carbohydrate: 19G; Fiber: .7G; Sodium: 240MG; Cholesterol: 7.1MG; Calories: 134.**

PUMPKIN BISQUE

Get into the spirit of the holiday with this creamy, richly colored soup. Pumpkin is the star, adding flavor, body, and a beautiful terra-cotta color. Serve with dark rye bread for a satisfying vegetarian entrée.

MAKES 6 SERVINGS

- 1 tablespoon butter
- 1 medium-size onion, chopped
- 1 stalk celery, chopped
- 1 medium-size carrot, peeled and chopped
- 1 medium-size potato, peeled and chopped
- 1 clove garlic, chopped
- 4½ cups water
- 1 teaspoon salt
- 1 16-ounce can pumpkin puree
- ¼ cup honey
- 1 tablespoon peeled chopped fresh gingerroot
- 1 cup milk

1 In a 4-quart saucepan, melt the butter over medium heat. Add the onion, celery, carrot, and potato and sauté for 5 minutes. Add the garlic and sauté 5 minutes longer. Stir in the water and salt; heat to boiling. Reduce the heat to low, cover, and simmer for 30 minutes.

2 Stir the pumpkin, honey, and gingerroot into the soup; cook, uncovered and stirring occasionally, for 20 minutes. Stir in the milk.

3 In batches, transfer the soup to a blender and puree. Transfer to a clean saucepan and gently reheat before serving.

NUTRITION PER SERVING **Protein: 3.2G; Fat: 3.5G; Carbohydrate: 27.8G; Fiber: 3.4G; Sodium: 435.5MG; Cholesterol: 9.2MG; Calories: 145.**

SPICY THREE-BEAN CHILI

- 2 tablesoons vegetable oil

- 2 medium-size onions, coarsely chopped

- 3 cloves garlic, finely chopped

- 2 28-ounce cans crushed tomatoes

- 2 16-ounce cans red kidney beans, undrained

- 2 16-ounce cans black beans, undrained

- 1 16-ounce can chickpeas, undrained

- 2 tablespoons ground cumin

- 1 to 2 tablespoons chili powder

- 1 to 2 tablespoons hot red-pepper sauce

- ½ teaspoon ground black pepper

- hot rice or warm corn tortillas

This super-quick version of the all-American favorite is a warming dish for hungry goblins returning from trick-or-treating. Go easy on the hot red-pepper sauce if you're feeding pint-sized party-goers.

MAKES 12 SERVINGS

Heat the oil in a 5-quart saucepan or Dutch oven over medium heat. Add the onions and garlic; sauté for 10 to 15 minutes, or until the onions are golden. Stir in the tomatoes, kidney beans, black beans, chickpeas, cumin, chili powder, red-pepper sauce, and black pepper. Heat to boiling. Serve over rice or with warm tortillas.

NUTRITION PER SERVING   Protein: 12.9G; Fat: 3.6G; Carbohydrate: 40.8G; Fiber: 11.7G; Sodium: 807.2MG; Cholesterol: 0MG; Calories: 238.

MINI CORN DOGS

1²/₃ cups all-purpose flour

¹/₃ cup yellow cornmeal

1 tablespoon baking powder

1 teaspoon salt

3 tablespoons cold margarine or butter

1 tablespoon shortening

³/₄ cup whole milk

1 16-ounce package miniature frankfurters (about 48 frankfurters), drained and patted dry

ketchup and mustard (optional)

In the early 1940s at the Texas State fair Neil Fletcher invented the "corny dog," a sausage on a stick, dipped in corn bread batter and fried. This oven-baked version is a treat for kids of all ages.

MAKES ABOUT 48 CORN DOGS

1 In a large bowl, stir together the flour, cornmeal, baking powder, and salt. With a pastry blender or 2 knives used scissor-fashion, cut in the margarine and shortening until the mixture resembles coarse crumbs. With a spoon, stir in the milk, a few tablespoons at a time, until the mixture forms a soft dough that leaves the side of the bowl.

2 Turn the dough onto a lightly floured surface; knead gently 4 to 5 times just until smooth. With a floured rolling pin, roll the dough into a 14-inch round about ¹/₈ inch thick.

3 Preheat the oven to 450°F. With a floured 2¹/₂-inch round biscuit cutter, cut out as many rounds as possible. Press the trimmings together; wrap with plastic wrap and set aside.

4 Place 1 frankfurter on each dough round. Bring the sides of the dough up and around the frankfurter; pinch in the center to seal; repeat. Place the wrapped frankfurters, seam sides up, 1¹/₂ inches apart, on a large ungreased baking sheet. Bake the corn dogs for 12 to 15 minutes, or until the biscuits are golden.

5 Reroll the trimmings ¹/₈ inch thick, and cut out additional rounds. Repeat step 4 with remaining frankfurters and dough rounds.

6 Serve warm with ketchup and mustard if you like.

NUTRITION PER PIECE **Protein: 2G; Fat: 4G; Carbohydrate: 5G; Fiber: 0G; Sodium: 180MG; Cholesterol: 6MG; Calories: 60.**

BAKED MACARONI WITH THREE CHEESES

A welcome main dish for kids and vegetarians alike. For a festive side dish, bake this recipe in individual 8-ounce ramekins.

1 pound rotini or cavatappi

2 cups whole milk

8 ounces cream cheese

3 tablespoons butter

1 teaspoon ground black pepper

½ teaspoon salt

1½ cups grated sharp Cheddar (about 6 ounces)

1½ cups shredded smoked Gouda (about 6 ounces)

MAKES 8 SERVINGS

1 Preheat the oven to 350°F. Cook the pasta following package directions. Strain the pasta, rinse with cold water to cool and prevent clumping, drain well, and transfer to a large bowl. Set aside. Combine the milk, cream cheese, butter, pepper, and salt in a medium saucepan. Cook over medium heat, stirring occasionally, until the butter and cream cheese have melted— about 10 minutes.

2 Toss the Cheddar and Gouda with the reserved pasta. Add the hot milk mixture and stir until well combined. Transfer pasta to a 3-quart baking dish and bake until the macaroni is set and the top is golden brown—about 30 minutes. Serve hot.

NUTRITION PER SERVING   protein: 18.4G; Fat: 30.4G; Carbohydrate: 20.6G; Fiber: .8G; Sodium: 583MG; Cholesterol: 102MG; Calories: 429.

APPLE-AND-SAGE-ROASTED CHICKEN

Nothing says "autumn" like a juicy roasted chicken. Add apple-and-sage stuffing and a whole-grain mustard rub and you guarantee contented guests.

MAKES 6 SERVINGS

- 1 4-pound roasting chicken
- ¾ teaspoon salt
- 3 medium apples, cored and quartered
- 3 small onions
- 2 ribs celery
- 2 cloves garlic
- 2 tablespoons chopped fresh sage
- ¼ cup (½ stick) butter, softened
- 1 tablespoon whole-grain mustard
- ⅛ teaspoon cracked white pepper
- 1 teaspoon chopped fresh thyme
- ¼ cup fruity white wine, such as Riesling
- ¾ cup fresh apple cider

1 Preheat the oven to 375°F. Rub the inside of the chicken with ½ teaspoon salt. Chop 1 apple, 1 onion, and the celery into 2-inch pieces. Toss the apple mixture with the garlic and 1 tablespoon sage, and place it all in the chicken cavity. Tie the legs together with kitchen twine, and tuck the wings securely under. Mix the butter and mustard to a smooth paste and rub over the chicken skin, reserving some for basting. Sprinkle with the remaining ¼ teaspoon salt and the white pepper.

2 Place the bird in a medium roasting pan. Roast in the lower third of the oven for 30 minutes. Brush the remaining mustard butter over the bird and continue to roast for 1¼ more hours. Baste the chicken with the pan drippings, and sprinkle with the remaining 1 tablespoon sage and the thyme. Halve then scatter the remaining apples and onions around the bird, tossing lightly to coat with the drippings. Add the white wine, and toast the chicken for 20 minutes. Baste the bird, and toss the apples and onions again for even browning. Continue to roast until bird juices run clear and the meat between the leg and thigh reaches 160°F. Remove from the oven and transfer the chicken to a serving platter. Arrange the apples and onions around the chicken.

3 Tip the roasting pan so the liquid pools to one end, and use a large spoon to remove any excess fat from the pan juices. Add apple cider and place the pan over medium-high heat. Use a wooden spoon to scrape the bottom of the pan, and then pour the jus over the chicken, apples, and onions. Serve warm.

NUTRITION PER SERVING   **Protein: 65.7G; Fat: 17.6G; Carbohydrate: 8.7G; Fiber: 2.3G; Sodium: 547MG; Cholesterol: 232MG; Calories: 511.**

WILD RICE- AND VENISON-STUFFED SUGAR PUMPKIN

You can make this recipe with venison or lean ground beef. Be sure to get an eating pumpkin (called "pie," "sweet," or "sugar pumpkin") for this savory treat; jack-o'-lantern pumpkins are not very tasty. Save the seeds to make Roasted Pumpkin Seeds (page 109).

- 1½ cups water
- ½ cup wild rice
- 1 teaspoon salt
- 1 4- to 5-pound sugar or other eating pumpkin
- 2 teaspoons vegetable oil
- 1 pound ground venison or lean ground beef
- ½ cup chopped green onions
- 1 teaspoon crushed dried sage
- ¼ teaspoon ground black pepper

MAKES 6 SERVINGS

1 In a 1-quart saucepan, heat the water to boiling over high heat. Stir in the wild rice and ½ teaspoon salt. Return to boiling. Cover; reduce the heat to low, and cook 40 to 45 minutes, or until the rice is tender and all the water is absorbed.

2 Preheat the oven to 350°F. Cut the top off the pumpkin and discard. Remove the seeds and fibers from center. Save the seeds for roasting or discard. Set the pumpkin in ½ inch water in a shallow roasting pan.

3 In a large skillet, heat the oil over medium-high heat. Add the meat and sauté until browned. Remove the skillet from the heat. Stir in the cooked wild rice, all but 1 tablespoon of the green onions, the sage, the remaining ½ teaspoon salt, and the pepper. Spoon the meat mixture into the pumpkin and cover the top with aluminum foil.

4 Bake the stuffed pumpkin for 45 to 60 minutes, or until tender when pierced with a fork. During baking, add more water to the roasting pan if necessary to keep the pumpkin from sticking.

5 Transfer the pumpkin to a serving dish; remove the foil and sprinkle with the remaining 1 tablespoon green onions. To serve, cut the pumpkin into wedges. Place a wedge with stuffing on each plate.

NUTRITION PER SERVING **Protein: 20.1G; Fat: 7.2G; Carbohydrate: 21.6G; Fiber: 3.4G; Sodium: 447.5MG; Cholesterol: 60.5MG; Calories: 227.**

PINEAPPLE-GLAZED HAM

More than enough to feed a crowd, this ham can be the centerpiece of a buffet at a large, spooky party or open house. Kids will love the pineapple glaze, which is not too sweet for adults.

1 12- to 14-pound fully cooked smoked ham

whole cloves

1 10-ounce jar pineapple preserves

1 tablespoon brown prepared mustard

1½ 8-ounce cans pineapple slices, drained

mint sprigs

MAKES 20 OR MORE SERVINGS

1 Preheat the oven to 325°F. Remove the skin and excess fat from the ham, leaving a layer of fat about ¼ inch thick. Score the fat layer into diamonds and insert a clove in the center of each diamond. Place the ham in a roasting pan and bake for 1½ hours.

2 In a small bowl, combine the preserves and mustard; brush 1 or 2 tablespoons over the ham. Make one cut through each pineapple slice. Place the pineapple on the ham, interlocking the slices to make a chain. Bake the ham 1 hour longer, brushing with the glaze often. Transfer the ham to a carving board and garnish with mint sprigs.

nutrition per serving **Protein: 277.3G; Fat: 13.7G; Carbohydrate: 12.7G; Fiber: .2G; Sodium: 2043.4MG; Cholesterol: 81.1MG; Calories: 284.**

"for grown-ups only" halloween fête

While some may still consider October 31st a children's holiday, each year more and more adults are getting into the All Hallows' Eve spirit. Whether you choose to throw an eerie, Gothic-themed night, a kitschy spook-fest featuring vintage costumes and retro decorations, or a warm and welcoming autumn fête as depicted here, your guests will appreciate a festive, "for grown-ups only" Halloween celebration.

Selecting the right space will go a long way toward creating the perfect party ambiance. If you're going for spooky, there's spine-tingling atmosphere galore in a musty basement, garage, or old barn. If the weather is too cold for these settings, it's not difficult to turn your house into a haunted one that will appeal to adult sensibilities. For a highly dramatic entrance, do as the Victorians did and let fire shed the only light, with jack-o'-lanterns by the front door, a fire in the fireplace, and candles everywhere.

[cont. on page 146]

Creepy Films

Consider playing one of these **classic horror movies** at your party:

* *The Black Castle*, 1952
* *The Black Cat*, 1934
* *Dr. Jekyll and Mr. Hyde*, 1920
* *The Exorcist*, 1973
* *Fall of the House of Usher*, 1960
* *Freaks*, 1932
* *The Haunting*, 1963
* *The Lost Boys*, 1987
* *Nosferatu*, 1922
* *Phantom of the Opera*, 1925
* *The Pit and the Pendulum*, 1961
* *The Raven*, 1935
* *Rosemary's Baby*, 1968
* *The Shining*, 1980
* *Interview with the Vampire*, 1994

All Hallows' Eve Dinner

Every item in this casual but decidedly grown-up menu **celebrates autumn's bounty**, from the apple-and-sage-stuffed chicken to the pumpkin-and-pecan-laced cake.

Harvest Moon Cocktail, page 105

Red Pear, Grape, and Pecan Salad, page 125

Apple-and-Sage-Roasted Chicken, page 138

Maple-Pecan Sweet Potatoes, page 131

Indian Shuck Bread, page 129

Golden Pumpkin Cake with Honey and Spice Buttercream, page 167

Ginger Crisps, page 152

White Spiced Coffee, page 107

ABOVE, FROM LEFT TO RIGHT: For rustic autumn charm, decorate your home with Indian corn and other seasonal bounty. Why not ice your guests' names on pear-shaped Ginger Crisps, center? That way, once they've located their seats, they can nibble on their placeholders—a prelude to a moist slice of Golden Pumpkin Cake with Honey and Spice Buttercream for dessert. OPPOSITE PAGE: A sun-dappled porch is the perfect setting for a Halloween dinner. The fanciful bower of corn and bittersweet frames a well-worn table set to showcase fall's plenty. Mismatched chairs from a flea market add to the casual atmosphere.

See Ghastly Books and Creepy Films (below and page 142) for inspiration; you may choose to create a theme party based on one of these eerie classics.

If instead you choose to throw a cozy, autumn dinner party, select a rustic setting as shown on page 145, or create a rustic look—you don't need to live in a farmhouse! Begin by setting a casual table with an unfussy table runner and ceramic dishes. Display a selection of pumpkins and gourds for the centerpiece and place settings. (See Mini-Pumpkin Placecards and Pumpkins as Art, pages 83 and 86, for ideas.) Outdoors, on a patio, would be charming if weather permits, but a leisurely meal in your dining room will be just as enjoyable. Decorating with Indian corn and other gifts from the autumn harvest will create a down-to-earth, country feel even if you live in the city. Turn the page for the perfect menu, which features hearty, seasonal fare and finishes with a delightfully fragrant spice cake and spiced coffee, too.

Ghastly Books

Look to these **literary thrillers** and **creepy ghost stories** for party themes and inspiration:

* Washington Irving's "The Legend of Sleepy Hollow" is the quintessential American ghost story and can be found in many anthologies, including *The Sketchbook* (Signet Press)

* For kids 9 and up, read *Scary Stories to Tell in the Dark*, by Alvin Schwartz (HarperCollins)

* *12 Gothic Tales*, edited by Richard Dalby (Oxford University Press)

* *Classic Chillers*, edited by E. M. Freeman (Globe Pequot Press)

* *12 Irish Ghost Stories*, edited by Patricia Craig (Oxford University Press)

* *18 Best Stories by Edgar Allan Poe*, edited by Chandler Brossard (Dell Publishing)

* *100 Hair-Raising Little Horror Stories*, selected by Al Sarrantonio & Martin H. Greenberg (Sterling Publishing Co.)

* *The Hound of the Baskervilles*, by Sir Arthur Conan Doyle

* *Frankenstein, or, The Modern Prometheus*, by Mary Shelley

* *Native American Ghost Stories*, by Darren Zenko and Amos Gideon (Lone Pine Publishing)

* *Campfire Stories, Volumes I-III*, edited by William W. Forgey, M.D. (Globe Pequot Press)

Carefully conceived invitations will help set the tone for your grown-up Halloween party. If you're throwing a small autumn dinner party, handmade invites can be attached to miniature pumpkins and left on doorsteps. If you're throwing a larger celebration with distinctly spooky overtones, consider making your own block-printed invitations with a Gothic theme; find an appropriately haunting illustration you can copy and see Boo-tiful Block-print Invitations, page 72, for instructions. Giving your party a name makes it extra-special, whether you chose to call it "All Hallows' Eve Dinner Party" or a "Gothic Fête for Grown-up Spirits."

Set up a bar with Halloween-appropriate brews such as cider, lager, black currant juice, and absinthe, and be ready to mix some creepy drinks, like a Snakebite, made with equal parts cider and lager. Or keep it simple and serve wine plus a single signature cocktail, such as the Harvest Moon Cocktail included in our menu.

When it's time for party games, gather around the fireplace. If it's a costume party, hold a costume contest, with the scariest, most original, and most ridiculous entries taking home prizes. Bob for apples and play pass-the-orange—you can't use your hands and the orange is tucked under your chin; the last person not to drop the orange wins. Or for a more sedate crowd, start a ghost story-telling round by giving each guest a twig. To begin, one person comes up with the opening sentence of a creepy story. A guest then throws a twig into the fire and continues the story until the twig is gone. Then the next guest throws his twig into the fire, taking up the thread of the tale.

festive baked goods

MOLASSES COOKIES

These spicy cookies are topped with a creamy, lemony frosting. Need a shortcut? Spread this frosting on store-bought cookies for an almost-homemade dessert.

1 cup (2 sticks) butter, room temperature; plus 2 tablespoons, softened

1 cup granulated sugar

1 cup molasses

1 cup sour cream

2 teaspoons ground ginger

½ teaspoon salt

3 teaspoons baking soda

3 tablespoons white vinegar

3 eggs, beaten

4 cups sifted all-purpose flour

2 cups packed confectioners' sugar, sifted

5½ tablespoons milk, warm; plus 3 tablespoons, very hot

1 teaspoon lemon extract

MAKES 40 COOKIES

1 Bake the cookies: Preheat the oven to 350°F. Beat the cup of butter and the granulated sugar until light and fluffy. Beat in the molasses, sour cream, ginger, and salt. Combine the baking soda and vinegar in a small bowl (it will fizz), and add to the butter mixture. Stir in the eggs and flour. Place a heaping tablespoon of dough per cookie, 2 inches apart, on a parchment paper–lined baking sheet. Bake until a toothpick inserted in the center comes out clean—about 15 minutes. Transfer the pan to a wire rack to cool completely before frosting.

2 Make the frosting: Beat the confectioners' sugar, 5½ tablespoons warm milk, and remaining 2 tablespoons warm butter together using a wooden spoon. Stir in the lemon extract. Add the remaining 3 tablespoons hot milk and beat until smooth. Use immediately to frost the cookies. Spread 1 teaspoon frosting on top of each cookie. Let frosting set before serving.

NUTRITION PER SERVING **Protein: 2G; Fat: 7G; Carbohydrate: 27G; Fiber: 0G; Sodium: 80MG; Cholesterol: 30MG; Calories: 180.**

JACK-O'-LANTERN COOKIES

Create a spooky parade of jack-o'-lantern cookies with pumpkin cookie cutters and royal icing. Meringue powder, specialty cookie cutters, and paste food coloring (which is more intense than liquid coloring) are available at cake decorating stores or online.

¾ cup granulated sugar

½ cup (1 stick) butter, softened

1 large egg

1 teaspoon vanilla extract

2 cups unsifted all-purpose flour

¼ teaspoon baking powder

¼ teaspoon salt

1 1-pound package (3½ cups) confectioners' sugar

3 large egg whites or equivalent amount of meringue powder mixed with water according to package directions

½ teaspoon cream of tartar

orange, green, and black paste food coloring

MAKES 2 TO 3 DOZEN COOKIES

1 In a medium-size bowl, with an electric mixer on medium speed, beat the granulated sugar and butter until light and fluffy. Beat in the egg and vanilla until well mixed. Reduce the speed to low and gradually beat in the flour, baking powder, and salt. Gather the dough into a ball, flatten into a 5-inch round, and wrap in plastic wrap. Refrigerate the dough for at least 30 minutes or overnight.

2 Preheat the oven to 325°F. Lightly grease 2 baking sheets. Cut 2 pieces of waxed paper the same size as the baking sheets. Cut the dough round in half. Wrap and return one piece to the refrigerator.

3 Lightly flour the waxed paper and roll out the dough between the paper to a ⅛-inch thickness. Remove the top piece of waxed paper from the dough. With different sizes of pumpkin cookie cutters, cut out as many cookies as possible, leaving at least a ½-inch space between them. Remove the trimmings and press together to reuse. Invert the waxed paper with the shapes onto a greased baking sheet. Peel off the waxed paper. Reroll the dough trimmings between the floured waxed paper and cut out more shapes. Invert the paper onto the second baking sheet; peel off the paper.

4 Bake the cookies for 10 to 14 minutes (depending on size), or until just golden at the edges. Cool for 5 minutes on the baking sheets; transfer to wire racks and cool completely.

5 Repeat Steps 3 and 4 with the remaining dough, using additional sheets of waxed paper, if necessary.

6 Prepare the royal icing: In a large bowl, with an electric mixer on low speed, beat the confectioners' sugar, egg whites, and cream of tartar until mixed. Increase the speed to high and beat about 5 minutes, or until very thick and fluffy. Cover tightly with plastic wrap to prevent drying until ready to use.

7 Transfer some of the frosting to 2 small bowls and color with the black and green food coloring. Cover with plastic wrap. Color the remaining frosting orange. Transfer some of the orange frosting to a medium-size bowl and beat in a few tablespoons of water until it reaches a spreadable consistency.

8 Spread the orange frosting on the cooled cookies with the back of a spoon. Let dry completely.

9 Transfer the orange frosting in the large bowl to a pastry bag fitted with a #1 tip. Use to pipe lines and dots on the cookies, leaving space in the middle of some to make jack-o'-lantern faces.

10 Repeat Step 9 with the green and black frosting, making stems and facial features.

- -

nutrition per cookie   **Protein: 1.5G; Fat: 3.3G; Carbohydrate: 26.6G; Fiber: .2G; Sodium: 53.9MG; Cholesterol: 15.2MG; Calories: 140.**

- -

GINGER CRISPS

Cookies make sweet placecards. Find decorating icing in the baking section of grocery stores. Cool completely before writing names with icing.

MAKES ABOUT 14 DOZEN COOKIES

1 cup butter (2 sticks), softened

½ cup firmly packed dark brown sugar

½ cup granulated sugar

⅓ cup molasses

⅔ cup light corn syrup

4½ cups sifted all-purpose flour

1½ teaspoons ground cinnamon

1½ teaspoons ground ginger

1 teaspoon salt

1 teaspoon baking powder

½ teaspoon ground cloves

1 Preheat the oven to 350°F. Beat the butter and sugars together, using a mixer on medium speed, until light and fluffy. Beat in the molasses and corn syrup until well combined. Add in the remaining ingredients and stir until a smooth dough forms. Chill for 30 minutes.

2 Roll out on a lightly floured surface to less than ⅛ inch thick. Cut with floured cookie cutters, such as the maple-leaf shapes shown at left. Bake on a greased cookie sheet for 8 minutes.

NUTRITION PER COOKIE **Protein: 0G; Fat: 1G; Carbohydrate: 4G; Fiber: 0G; Sodium: 20MG; Cholesterol: 5MG; Calories: 30.**

Freezing Extra Dough

This recipe will yield an abundance of cookies, which you may not need right away. Roll unused dough into logs, wrap well, and freeze for up to one month.

PUMPKIN CHEESECAKE

A great do-ahead Halloween dessert, this treat can be made the day before the party.

- ⅓ cup butter or margarine
- 1½ cups gingersnap cookie crumbs
- 2 8-ounce packages cream cheese, softened
- ½ cup granulated sugar
- ½ cup canned or fresh pumpkin puree
- ½ teaspoon ground cinnamon
- ½ teaspoon ground cloves
- ½ teaspoon ground nutmeg
- 2 large eggs
- ½ teaspoon vanilla extract

MAKES 8 SERVINGS

1 Prepare the gingersnap crust: In a small saucepan, melt the butter over low heat. Remove from heat and stir in the cookie crumbs until well mixed. Press the mixture firmly onto the bottom of a 9-inch springform pan and set aside.

2 Preheat the oven to 350°F. Prepare the pumpkin cheesecake filling: In a large bowl, with an electric mixer on medium speed, beat the cream cheese, sugar, pumpkin, cinnamon, cloves, and nutmeg until combined. Beat in the eggs and vanilla until well mixed. Pour into the crust.

3 Bake for 40 to 45 minutes, or until the center is almost set. Cool on a wire rack to room temperature. Cover and refrigerate for 3 hours or overnight.

4 Just before serving, remove the rim of the pan and place the cheesecake on a serving plate.

nutrition per serving   **Protein: 7G; Fat: 30.2G; Carbohydrate: 27.2G; Fiber: .9G; Sodium: 338.4MG; Cholesterol: 135.4MG; Calories: 401.**

CHEESECAKE BROWNIES

Topped with cream cheese frosting and swirls of pumpkin butter, these are no ordinary brownies. And to please the eye further, you can transform them into holiday-inspired shapes with cookie cutters, available at specialty baking stores or online. For best results, chill brownies before cutting shapes.

- 1½ cups (3 sticks) butter
- ¾ pound bittersweet chocolate, chopped
- 8 large eggs
- 1½ cups firmly packed dark brown sugar
- 2 cups granulated sugar
- 4 teaspoons vanilla extract
- 1½ teaspoons salt
- 2½ cups all-purpose flour
- ¾ cup cocoa
- 2 8-ounce packages cream cheese, softened
- 2 tablespoons cornstarch
- 1 cup apricot jam
- 1 cup pumpkin butter

MAKES 3 DOZEN BROWNIES

1 Preheat the oven to 325°F. Line a baking pan with parchment paper and lightly butter. Melt the butter and chocolate in the top of a double boiler. Whisk 6 eggs, brown sugar, and 1½ cups granulated sugar together. Stir in 3 teaspoons vanilla, salt, melted chocolate, flour, and cocoa. Pour into the prepared pan.

2 Beat cream cheese using a mixer on medium speed until fluffy. Add the remaining 2 eggs, ½ cup sugar, 1 teaspoon vanilla, and the cornstarch; beat until smooth and spread over the chocolate batter.

3 Combine jam and pumpkin butter. Drop in spoonfuls onto the cream cheese and draw swirls using a knife. Bake until center tests clean—about 40 minutes. Cool before removing from the pan, then punch out shapes using Halloween-themed cutters if desired.

NUTRITION PER SERVING   **Protein: 7G; Fat: 21G; Carbohydrate: 40G; Fiber: 2G; Sodium: 160MG; Cholesterol: 75MG; Calories: 348.**

{ VARIATIONS }

Frosting Alternatives: In place of pumpkin butter, swirl peanut butter, apple butter, or raspberry jam into the cheesecake topping.

Mix-Ins: Stir chocolate or peanut butter chips into the batter before baking. Or add chopped nuts, such as walnuts, pecans, or hazelnuts.

Shapes: Instead of using themed cutters, slice the brownies into triangles. First cut them into squares or rectangles, then cut each shape on the diagonal.

CRANBERRY-APPLE CRISP

4 large green apples, peeled, cored, and sliced ½ inch thick

1 cup fresh cranberries

¾ cup firmly packed dark brown sugar

½ cup all-purpose flour

½ cup rolled oats

¾ teaspoon ground cinnamon

¾ teaspoon ground nutmeg

⅓ cup butter, softened

ice cream or whipped cream

Be ready to bake a crisp any time. Make a large batch of the crumb topping, but omit the butter until you are ready to use. Store in an airtight container.

MAKES 6 SERVINGS

1 Preheat the oven to 375°F. Lightly coat an 8-inch-square baking pan with butter. Add apples and cranberries to the pan. Combine the brown sugar, flour, oats, cinnamon, nutmeg, and softened butter in a bowl. Sprinkle over the fruit.

2 Bake until golden brown—about 30 minutes. Serve hot with ice cream or cold with whipped cream.

nutrition per serving   **Protein: 4G; Fat: 11G; Carbohydrate: 57G; Fiber: 4G; Sodium: 15MG; Cholesterol: 25MG; Calories: 330.**

AUTUMN FRUIT PIE

2 cups unsifted all-purpose flour

½ teaspoon salt

½ cup (1 stick) butter

¼ cup vegetable shortening

4 to 5 tablespoons cold water

10 Granny Smith apples, peeled, cored, and thinly sliced

1 cup pitted dates, chopped

1 cup fresh cranberries

½ cup granulated sugar

1 tablespoon lemon juice

1 teaspoon ground cinnamon

½ teaspoon ground nutmeg

Celebrate the harvest with this flavorful offering. Dates and cranberries impart natural sweetness and tart flavor to a generous apple filling.

MAKES 10 SERVINGS

1 Prepare the pastry: In a medium-size bowl, combine the flour and salt. With a pastry blender or 2 knives, cut the butter and shortening into the flour mixture until the mixture resembles coarse crumbs. One tablespoon at a time, sprinkle the water over the flour mixture and mix lightly until the pastry holds together. Shape the pastry into 2 equal balls and flatten each to a 1-inch thickness. Wrap and refrigerate for 30 minutes.

2 Prepare the fruit filling: In a 5-quart saucepan, combine the apples, dates, cranberries, sugar, lemon juice, cinnamon, and nutmeg. Heat to boiling over medium heat, stirring frequently. Cook about 20 minutes, or until the apples are soft but still retain their shape.

3 Preheat the oven to 400°F. Between 2 sheets of floured waxed paper, roll out one ball of pastry to an 11-inch round. Remove the top sheet of paper and invert the pastry onto a 9-inch pie plate, letting excess extend over the edge. Remove the remaining sheet of waxed paper. Spoon the apple filling onto the pastry.

4 Roll out the remaining pastry to a 12-inch round to make the top crust. Remove the top sheet of paper and invert the pastry over the filling. Remove the paper; gently press the pastries around the rim where they meet. Carefully fold the edge of the top crust under the edge of the bottom crust, making a soft rolled border. Cut 4 slits in the top to allow steam to escape during baking.

5 Bake the pie for 30 to 35 minutes, or until the pastry is golden brown. Cool on a wire rack for 15 to 20 minutes before serving.

NUTRITION PER SERVING **Protein: 3.6G; Fat: 14.5G; Carbohydrate: 64.1G; Fiber: 4.9G; Sodium: 182.5MG; Cholesterol: 24.4MG; Calories: 385.**

FALLING LEAVES PUMPKIN PIE

2 frozen deep-dish pie shells

1½ cups canned or fresh pumpkin puree

1 cup heavy cream

¾ cup firmly packed light brown sugar

½ cup whole milk

2 large eggs

1 large egg yolk

1 tablespoon maple syrup

1 tablespoon pumpkin-pie spice

½ teaspoon salt

granulated sugar, for glazing pastry leaves

Shhhhh. This pastry isn't homemade. And the pastry oak leaves are baked on a sheet pan. Before slicing the pie, remove the leaves, then replace them on guests' plates.

MAKES 9 SERVINGS

1 Preheat the oven to 425°F. Remove one pie shell from its pan, and thaw completely, in the refrigerator, on a parchment-lined sheet pan. Bake the remaining pie shell for 10 minutes and cool completely on a wire rack.

2 Combine the pumpkin puree, cream, brown sugar, milk, eggs, egg yolk, maple syrup, pumpkin-pie spice, and salt in a large bowl, stirring until smooth. Fill the baked pie shell. Bake for 15 minutes, reduce heat to 350°F, and continue to bake until set—about 40 minutes longer. Cool completely on a wire rack.

3 Meanwhile, trim away the crimped edge of the thawed pie shell and gently flatten with a rolling pin. Cut out 15 leaf shapes using mini (½-inch) cookie cutters dipped in flour. Etch "vein lines" on leaves. Lightly brush with water, sprinkle on sugar, and bake at 350°F on a sheet pan until golden brown. Arrange the cooled leaves around the pie's rim.

nutrition per serving **Protein: 3.7G; Fat: 15.6G; Carbohydrate: 31.9G; Fiber: 1G; Sodium: 242MG; Cholesterol: 89MG; Calories: 279.**

BOURBON WHIPPED CREAM

1 cup heavy cream

2 teaspoons confectioners' sugar

1 tablespoon bourbon

Whipped cream and pumpkin pie are inseparable. Here's a festive variation that no one can resist.

MAKES 8 SERVINGS

1 Chill a mixing bowl and beaters or whisk for 20 minutes.

2 Beat or whisk the cream, confectioners' sugar, and bourbon until soft peaks form.

3 Transfer the flavored whipped cream to a serving bowl, or dollop directly onto slices of Falling Leaves Pumpkin Pie.

NUTRITION PER 2 TABLESPOONS **Protein: .4G; Fat: 6G; Carbohydrate: 1G; Fiber: 0G; Sodium: 6MG; Cholesterol: 23MG; Calories: 63.**

Festive Pastry Leaves

These pastry leaves are not only pretty, they have the added advantage of hiding crust imperfections. For quick color, dot the leaves with fresh cranberries that you've coated with corn syrup and rolled in sugar, as shown in photo opposite.

MINI PUMPKIN SPICE CAKES

- ¾ cup (1½ sticks) butter, softened
- 1 cup firmly packed dark brown sugar
- 1 cup granulated sugar
- 3 large eggs
- ½ cup buttermilk
- 1 cup canned or fresh pumpkin puree
- 1 teaspoon vanilla extract
- 2 cups all-purpose flour
- 2 teaspoons baking powder
- 1 teaspoon baking soda
- 1½ teaspoons ground cinnamon
- ½ teaspoon fresh-ground nutmeg

To take these little cakes to a delicious new level, adapt the recipe with cocoa. Replace 3 tablespoons flour with ¼ cup sweetened cocoa. The result will be a delectable little cake, rich with chocolaty flavor and tinged with autumn baking spices. Or top each cake with a glaze or sparkly sugar: see variations below.

MAKES 12 SERVINGS

1 Preheat the oven to 350°F. Butter and flour 2 Bundtlette pans (6-cup capacity); set aside. This recipe also makes about 12 mini layers (4-ounce ramekins) or 15 jumbo muffin–size cakes.

2 Beat the butter in a large bowl, using a mixer set on medium speed, until fluffy. Beat in the sugars and eggs, one at a time, until smooth. Combine the buttermilk, pumpkin, and vanilla in a separate bowl and set aside.

3 In another bowl, combine the flour, baking powder, baking soda, cinnamon, and nutmeg and stir into batter in thirds—alternating with the buttermilk mixture—until smooth. Pour the batter into prepared pans.

4 Bake until the cakes test clean—about 25 minutes. Cool on wire racks.

NUTRITION PER SERVING   Protein: 2.2G; Fat: 6.5G; Carbohydrate: 26.5G; Fiber: 0G; Sodium: 102MG; Cholesterol: 42.5 MG; Calories: 170.

{ VARIATIONS }

Citrus Glaze: For a pumpkinlike color, combine 1¼ cups confectioners' sugar with 3 tablespoons lemon juice and tint with orange food coloring. Drizzle over cake with a spoon.

Vanilla Glaze: This sweet classic combines 1½ cups confectioners' sugar with 3 tablespoons water and ½ teaspoon vanilla. Drizzle over cake.

After cakes have been brushed lightly with corn syrup, they can be sprinkled with **pumpkin-colored sparkling sugar**.

GRANDMA'S APPLESAUCE CAKE

We'll let you in on Grandma's secret: for depth of flavor, add a little cocoa and fresh coffee to the batter.

- 2 cups all-purpose flour
- ½ cup cocoa powder
- 1 teaspoon baking soda
- 1 teaspoon baking powder
- ½ teaspoon salt
- 1½ teaspoons ground cinnamon
- 1 teaspoon ground allspice
- ¼ teaspoon ground cloves
- ½ cup (1 stick) butter
- 1½ cups firmly packed dark brown sugar
- 2 large eggs, at room temperature
- 1½ cups applesauce
- ¾ cup strongly brewed black coffee, hot
- 1½ cups black raisins
- ¾ cup chopped walnuts
- 2 cups confectioners' sugar

MAKES 10 SERVINGS

1 Make the batter: Preheat the oven to 350°F. Lightly butter and flour a 6-cup Kugelhof or Bundt pan. Whisk the flour, ¼ cup cocoa powder, baking soda, baking powder, salt, cinnamon, allspice, and cloves together in a large bowl and set aside. Cream the butter and brown sugar until light and fluffy in a large bowl using a mixer set at medium-high speed. Add 1 egg, beating just until incorporated. Repeat with remaining egg. Reduce mixer speed to low and add the flour mixture by thirds, alternating with the applesauce. Scrape down sides of bowl and increase mixer speed to medium. Quickly add ½ cup hot coffee, beating until thoroughly combined—about 30 seconds. Fold in the raisins and walnuts.

2 Bake the cake: Pour the batter into the prepared pan and bake on the middle rack of the oven until a tester inserted in the center comes out clean—40 to 45 minutes. Place the cake in pan on a wire rack and cool until slightly warm. Gently run a knife around the edge of the pan, turn out the cake, and cool completely.

3 Make the glaze: Sift powdered sugar and remaining cocoa powder together. Make a well in the center and quickly pour in the remaining ¼ cup hot coffee. Whisk until well blended and smooth. Pour over top of cake, allowing it to soak in. Serve immediately.

NUTRITION PER SERVING **Protein: 7.9G; Fat: 16.6G; Carbohydrate: 85.7G; Fiber: 3.9G; Sodium: 309MG; Cholesterol: 67.4MG; Calories: 494.**

tantalizing recipes & bewitching parties 161

EASY AUTUMN CAKES

1 chocolate cake mix (such as Duncan Hines Moist Deluxe Devil's Food Mix)

2 teaspoons pumpkin-pie spice

²/₃ cup canned or fresh pumpkin puree

³/₄ cup water

¹/₄ cup (½ stick) butter, softened

3 large eggs

1 cup finely ground pecans

One easy base recipe, three great cakes: the sensational tiered Pumpkin Patch Cake, opposite, the playful Great Pumpkin Cake, page 165, and the Golden Pumpkin Cake with Honey and Spice Buttercream shown on page 167.

MAKES 10 SERVINGS

1 Preheat the oven to 350°F. Lightly butter and flour either a 10-cup Great Pumpkin Pan or 3 round cake pans—6, 8, and 10 inches. (If making the tiered cake, plan also to double the recipe.) Take care to coat all crevices and corners.

2 Place all of the ingredients in a large mixing bowl and beat, using a mixer set on medium-high speed, until batter is smooth. Fill the cake pans. (For the Great Pumpkin Pan, divide batter evenly between the two halves; for the round cake pans, divide batter evenly.)

3 Bake until a skewer inserted into the center tests clean—about 35 minutes for the pumpkin cakes; 25 minutes for the 6-inch, 30 minutes for the 8-inch, and 35 minutes for the 10-inch layers of the tiered cake. Cool completely on a wire rack before frosting or decorating.

4 Trim the pumpkin cake halves before stacking together to form the pumpkin-shaped cake or stack tiers, spreading frosting between layers.

NUTRITION PER SERVING   Protein: 4.7G; Fat: 17.3G; Carbohydrate: 36.8G; Fiber: 2G; Sodium: 306MG; Cholesterol: 63.8MG; Calories: 315.

OPPOSITE: PUMPKIN PATCH CAKE

Pumpkin-Patch Cake

Bake an impression, but don't expect it to last. This towering pumpkin patch begins as three layers of Easy Autumn Cake (page 162) in graduated sizes, with three generous layers of Honey and Spice Buttercream (page 167). The pumpkins and leaves, both made of tinted marzipan, needn't be perfect to be appreciated, so invite young helpers to assist. See Marzipan Flourishes below.

{DECORATION}

Marzipan Flourishes: Divide the marzipan into three batches. With food coloring, tint one green and one orange; leave one natural. For mottling, combine batches. To make the marzipan stem and leaves, twist yourself a stem and cut out leaves with a cookie cutter. For the mini pumpkins, roll some orange spheres, score the lobes with a skewer, and top with perky green stems.

The Great Pumpkin Cake

With its vanilla-sugar icing and marzipan stem, this cake, also made using
Easy Autumn Cakes recipe (page 162) is sure to earn Best of Show. The secret
to its perfect form? A fluted, dome-shaped pan. The pumpkin shape is actually
composed of two dome-shaped cakes fitted together. Add the stem and leaf after
icing; see Easy Icing below and Marzipan Flourishes opposite.

{ DECORATION }

Easy Icing: Whisk 1 cup confectioners' sugar with 2 to 3 tablespoons
lemon juice until it's the consistency of molasses. Drizzle over the Great
Pumpkin Cake.

HONEY AND SPICE BUTTERCREAM

- 1 teaspoon unflavored gelatin
- 4 tablespoons water
- ½ cup dark honey
- ½ cup granulated sugar
- ½ teaspoon salt
- 2 teaspoons ground cinnamon
- 1¾ cups (3½ sticks) butter, at room temperature
- 1 teaspoon vanilla extract

You can prepare the frosting ahead. Chill it and rewhip before spreading on the cake.

MAKES 4 CUPS

1 Combine the gelatin and 2 tablespoons water and let sit for 10 minutes. Bring the honey, sugar, and remaining 2 tablespoons water to a boil in a small saucepan, reduce heat to low, and simmer for 5 minutes. Remove from heat and let cool for 3 minutes.

2 Stir 2 tablespoons of the honey mixture into the gelatin until dissolved. Whisk into the remaining honey syrup along with the salt and cinnamon.

3 Strain into a medium-size bowl and beat, using a mixer set on high speed, until doubled in volume and completely cool—about 10 minutes. Add the butter, 2 tablespoons at a time, while continuously beating. Stir in the vanilla and use immediately or keep chilled.

nutrition per 2 tablespoons **Protein: 0.2G; Fat: 8.5G; Carbohydrate: 7.7G; Fiber: 0.2G; Sodium: 38MG; Cholesterol: 23MG; Calories: 105.**

Golden Pumpkin Cake

Top this moist loaf cake (shown opposite) with a generous layer of Honey and Spice Buttercream. Follow the **Easy Autumn Cakes recipe** on page 162, but substitute Duncan Hines Moist Deluxe Butter Recipe Golden Mix. Decrease the water added to the batter to ⅔ cup. Bake in two 9-inch loaf pans for 35 minutes. Frost and serve.

DEVILISH CHOCOLATE CAKES

Cast a spell this Halloween with festive chocolate desserts—all made with a single foolproof cake recipe. Whether you choose to make cream-topped snack cakes, mini chocolate pumpkins, or layer cakes decorated with a spiderweb or a spooky, sparkly cat (see page 171), these fun treats are sure to satisfy.

- 2 cups all-purpose flour
- ½ cup cocoa
- 1 teaspoon baking powder
- 1 teaspoon baking soda
- 1 teaspoon salt
- ¾ cup (1½ sticks) butter, softened
- ⅓ cup granulated sugar
- ½ cup firmly packed dark brown sugar
- 3 eggs
- ¼ cup sour cream
- 2 teaspoons vanilla extract
- 1¼ cups milk

MAKES 18 FILLED CAKES, TWO 8-INCH-ROUND LAYERS, OR 12 MINI PUMPKINS

1 Preheat the oven to 350°F. Butter and flour three 6-cup muffin pans (for filled snack cakes), two 8-inch-round cake pans (for layer cake), or 2 mini Bundt pans (for Mini Pumpkin Cakes). Set aside.

2 Combine the flour, cocoa, baking powder, baking soda, and salt and set aside. Beat the butter and sugars together in a bowl using an electric mixer on medium-high speed. Beat in the eggs one at a time. Reduce speed to medium-low. Stir the sour cream, vanilla, and milk together and add it in thirds, alternating with the flour mixture. Beat until batter is smooth, about 3 more minutes.

3 Divide the batter equally between the prepared pans and bake until a wooden skewer inserted into the center tests clean. For the layer cake, it should take about 25 minutes; filled snack cakes, 20 minutes; and Mini Pumpkin Cakes, 25 minutes. Cool on a wire rack. Trim cooled cake layers, if necessary, to make level and frost and decorate as desired.

NUTRITION PER MUFFIN-SIZE CAKE Protein: 5.2G; Fat: 28.3G; Carbohydrate: 40.7G; Fiber: 2.2G; Sodium: 253MG; Cholesterol: 88MG; Calories: 255.

OPPOSITE: WICKED WEB CAKE

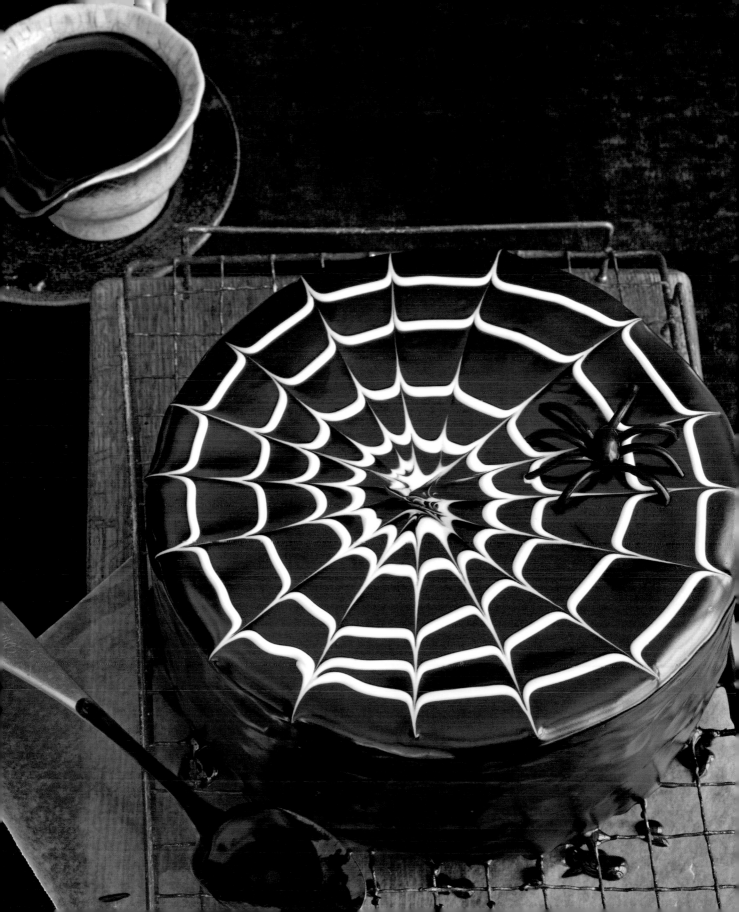

CHOCOLATE GLAZE

9 ounces bittersweet chocolate, finely chopped

1½ tablespoons butter

½ cup heavy cream

MAKES 1½ CUPS

Place the chocolate and butter together in a heatproof bowl; set aside. Heat the heavy cream until it just begins to boil and immediately pour over the chocolate. Stir gently until smooth. Let sit until slightly thickened before using to glaze cakes, about 3 minutes. Place the cakes in the refrigerator for 5 to 10 minutes to set the chocolate. For filled cakes: Pour chocolate on each filled cake and smooth over the cake to completely coat. Place the cakes in the freezer until chocolate sets. Remove and store in a cool area.

NUTRITION PER 2 TABLESPOONS   **Protein: 1.7G; Fat: 14G; Carbohydrate: 11G; Fiber: 1.5G; Sodium: 4MG; Cholesterol: 17.4MG; Calories: 153.**

VANILLA GLAZE

1 cup confectioners' sugar

2 to 3 tablespoons water

¼ teaspoon vanilla extract

orange food coloring (optional)

MAKES ½ CUP

Whisk the sugar and vanilla extract together with the water until the glaze is the consistency of molasses. Tint half the icing with orange food coloring until the desired color is reached and leave the remaining icing white. Drizzle 2 teaspoons of either white or orange glaze over each Mini Pumpkin Cake.

NUTRITION PER 2 TEASPOONS   **Protein: 0G; Fat: 0G; Carbohydrate: 10G; Fiber: 0G; Sodium: 0MG; Cholesterol: 0MG; Calories: 40.**

Decorating Magic
Sprinkle poppy seeds or coarse colored sugar on the glaze before it sets.

{ VARIATIONS }

Devilish Chocolate Cake and Vanilla Cream Filling (see pages 168 and 173) are only the beginning. Master a few decorating tricks and you can turn these already magical recipes into four truly enchanting cakes!

Bite-sized Snack Cakes with Vanilla Cream Filling:
Coat these cakes thoroughly with chocolate glaze. Orange food coloring, added one drop at a time, gives the cream stripe on top its brilliant hue. Use a pastry bag to pipe it on.

Mini Pumpkin Cakes with Marzipan Pumpkin Stems:
To make these single-serving treats, trim the bottoms of cakes baked in mini Bundt pans to create flat surfaces. Join two cakes so that the fluted tops are at either end, then drizzle the tops with Chocolate or Vanilla Glaze and sprinkle with coarse colored sugar or nonpareils before the glaze sets. Top with a marzipan stem; they are a cinch if you follow these steps: Start by dividing an 8-ounce can of marzipan into two batches. With food coloring, tint one batch yellow and the other light green. Roll the separate colors into small logs, then gently twine the two pieces together and roll lightly for a mottled look. Taper the green-and-yellow log at one end and coil it. To ensure that your stem stays put, anchor it to the cake with a toothpick.

Wicked Web Cake with White-Chocolate Spiderweb:
For a wickedly good web, pour Chocolate Glaze over the top of an uniced two-layer cake. Spread the glaze over the cake's edges and smooth the sides. Fill a small piping bag with 3 to 4 tablespoons of melted white chocolate, then starting at the center of the top of the cake, pipe white chocolate in a spiral. Drag a toothpick from the center of the spiral to the cake's edge. Repeat every 1½ inches to create a web effect.

Spooky Black Cat Cake with Fondant Stripes: Fill
and frost a two-layer cake with your favorite icing, leaving a smooth surface for decorations. Roll out black fondant into a ⅛-inch-thick sheet, and with a tape measure as a guide, cut three strips long enough to wrap around the cake's circumference; adhere using extra dabs of icing, if needed. Chill the cake. Meanwhile, photocopy and cut out the Spooky Black Cat stencil from the front cover of this book. Before serving, center the stencil on top of the cake and fill it in with black sanding sugar (available at baking specialty stores or online), leaving the edges a little messy for a spooky effect. Add a half a yellow M&M or other candy for the cat's eye.

VANILLA CREAM FILLING

Use this vanilla cream to fill the chocolate snack cakes. See photo opposite.

1 cup whole milk

2½ tablespoons all-purpose flour

1 cup (2 sticks) butter

1 cup confectioners' sugar

1 teaspoon vanilla extract

orange food coloring

MAKES 18 SERVINGS -

1 Whisk the milk and flour together in a medium saucepan. Cook over medium heat, whisking constantly, until thickened, about 5 minutes. Transfer to a bowl and cool to room temperature.

2 Beat the butter and sugar together in a bowl until fluffy. Beat in the vanilla and the milk mixture until smooth. Stir in the food coloring until blended and desired color.

3 Fit a pastry bag with a long, narrow tip and fill halfway with cream filling. Insert the tip into the trimmed cake bottoms and fill each. (Note: Cake will feel heavier in the hand after it is filled.) Use the remaining filling to decorate the tops of each glazed cake.

- -

nutrition per serving   **Protein: 5.2G; Fat: 28.3G; Carbohydrate: 40.7G; Fiber: 2.2G; Sodium: 253 MG; Cholesterol: 88MG; Calories: 255.**

- -

opposite: bite-sized snack cakes

the great pumpkin carving party

Bring friends and family together for a pumpkin-carving party filled with fun and games, food and good times for guests of all ages. Host the festivities outdoors, so everyone can revel in autumn's splendor (and you can avoid a living room full of pumpkin seeds and guts!). Begin the party in the late afternoon, but hang some paper lanterns or hurricane lamps to illuminate the festivities as dusk approaches. Keep it casual by using bales of straw, picnic tables, and lawn chairs for seating.

You should provide the pumpkins, but ask your guests to bring carving tools so there are plenty of knives and chisels for everyone. Carving should be restricted to adults, or well-supervised teens and 'tweens, but make sure kids feel welcome to participate by providing them with markers to draw jack-o'-lantern faces, along with fun embellishments, like glitter and pinecones, that they can easily glue onto their pumpkins. You might want to set up a few other activities to keep kids happily occupied, whether that's water-coloring or croquet or "pin the hat on the witch." Spooky Halloween music will keep everything festive and may inspire some guests to dance.

When all the work is done, display the jack-o'-lanterns on your porch or walkway, then invite everyone to sit back and enjoy a delicious buffet. We've provided a tempting menu of autumn-inspired fare to please kids and adults alike, but if you want to further minimize the fuss, make it a potluck. You can prepare a hearty main dish and drinks and assign the rest of the courses to your guests—or just invite them to bring a seasonal dish of some kind. No one will mind if desserts dominate!

Pumpkin-Carving Buffet

A buffet is convenient for the host and makes your guests feel at ease. You'll want to present a **mouthwatering selection** of comfort food and desserts, whether you follow this menu, or invite your guests to participate in a potluck.

Mulled Cider, page 106

Roasted Pumpkin Seeds, page 109

Caramel Apples, page 115

Pineapple-Glazed Ham, page 141

Acorn Squash Stuffed with Rutabaga and Pecans, page 132

Green Beans with Smoked Bacon and Onions, page 130

Sweet Potato Biscuits, page 133

Mini Pumpkin Spice Cakes, page 160

Cheesecake Brownie Cutouts, page 154

Jack-o'-Lantern Cookies, page 150

OPPOSITE PAGE: **For an especially memorable treat, dress up your caramel apples with nuts, sprinkles, and swirls of chocolate.**
ABOVE, FROM LEFT TO RIGHT: **Sweet Potato Biscuits, Acorn Squash Stuffed with Rutabaga and Pecans, and Mini Pumpkin Spice Cakes are all welcome additions to any Halloween buffet table.**

Planning Your Pumpkin Party

{INVITING: FOUR WEEKS BEFORE}

* Write **fun invitations**, get them in the mail, and ask guests to RSVP so you'll know how many to expect. If you think you might need a tent, order it now.

* If you want to organize a **potluck-style supper**, ask guests to bring their favorite fall dish to share. Ask them to let you know what course they plan to bring when they RSVP, so you have enough main dishes, desserts, and sides. (You can safely count on plenty of desserts.)

* Remind guests to **bring layers**, since the weather in late October can grow chilly suddenly.

{PREPARING: TWO WEEKS BEFORE}

* Ask a local farmers' market or produce store if they'll deliver pumpkins to your home. Make sure to order **one pumpkin per guest**, plus some extras, and don't forget to ask for a couple of smaller "pie" pumpkins" (they're ideal for children to decorate).

* Order or borrow any other items you'll need: tea lights or strings of holiday lights, paper lanterns or hurricane lamps, bales of straw or other seating, art supplies or other activities for the kids. Purchase paper cups, plates, tableware, and napkins, or gather together an adequate supply for all your guests. Be sure you'll have **enough serving pieces** for every item on the menu, and don't be shy about borrowing an ice bucket or punch bowl if you don't own one.

* Repurpose items lying unused in your garage or basement. An old folding table is an excellent place to arrange carving supplies, beverages, or a buffet, while upside-down buckets can double as **easy-to-transport seating**.

{ SETTING UP: THE DAY OF PARTY }

❋ Whether you're cooking the entire meal yourself or contributing a main dish and beverages to the potluck, make it easy on yourself by preparing everything ahead of time and rewarming, if necessary, at serving time. All serving pieces should be lined up and ready to go in your kitchen.

❋ Set up a **pumpkin-carving area** and consolidate sharp tools and matches or lighters in a container, where adults can supervise them. Include an Adults Only sign on the toolbox so everyone is aware of the rules. Include a second kid-friendly box filled with markers, glue, and trinkets kids can use to decorate pumpkins themselves.

❋ The chill of autumn nights can catch people by surprise. Gather old sweaters and shawls, hats and scarves and stow them in readily accessible baskets so your guests can borrow what they need.

❋ Designate containers for pumpkin pulp and return it to the earth as compost. The seeds can be used for **Roasted Pumpkin Seeds**, page 109. They take just 10 or 15 minutes to bake and make a delightfully crunchy-salty addition to your buffet table.

CHAPTER FOUR

ghoulish costumes & clever disguises

trick or treat?

Trick-or-treating is just as enduring an American folk tradition as pumpkin carving. Originating in ancient customs designed to scare the spirits of the underworld, these rituals are today simply part of an evening of fun. Though we no longer fear the supernatural, asking for treats by going from house to house in disguise on a dark, cold night is one way we honor our past. Whether you live in a rural area or a city, there are many tricks to making October 31st memorable. In many neighborhoods, the festivities begin at sundown, with a parade of children in colorful costumes that starts in a local park and eventually spills out onto the street. Parents receive a list of homes participating in trick-or-treating and then the fun begins. A jack-o'-lantern marks each door as children and their parents, often also in costume, parade from door to door, to be greeted by a witch or goblin holding out a basket of goodies.

We have the Victorians to thank for bringing back today's popular custom of dressing up in costumes and masks. They brought their genteel sensibilities to Halloween, diluting the ancient, darker practices of the night by inviting guests into their homes for a party. The parties were themed, and every guest was required to wear a clever costume. Toward the end of the 19th century, trick-or-treating became popular in the United States, its origins in the Irish practice of asking for food for the poor—good luck came to those who gave, mischief and bad luck threatened those who refused.

Haunted Happenings

There is nothing like **a visit to a haunted house**, spooky cemetery, or corn-stalk maze to get you and the kids in the Halloween spirit!

Winchester Mystery House

525 South Winchester Boulevard
San Jose, CA
408-247-2101
www.winchestermysteryhouse.com
Take a flashlight tour!

Mind-boggling Maze

Denver Botanic Gardens
1005 York Street
Denver, CO
720-865-3500
www.botanicgardens.org
Get lost in this gigantic maze
constructed from 12-foot stalks of
corn!

Lafayette #1 Cemetery

Washington Avenue and Sixth Street

St. Louis #1 Cemetery

425 Basin Street
New Orleans, LA
800-672-6124
St. Louis #1 is the oldest cemetery
in New Orleans. Visit the tomb of
Voodoo Priestess Marie Laveau.

Westminster Hall Burying Ground

Fayette and Greene Streets
Baltimore, MD
410-706-2072
www.westminsterhall.org
The city's oldest cemetery and final
resting place of Edgar Allan Poe, with
catacombs as well as the graveyard.

Salem Witch Museum

Washington Square North
Salem, MA
978-744-1692
www.salemwitchmuseum.org
Learn about the history of witches,
witchcraft, and witch hunts.

Procession of Ghouls

The Cathedral Church
of Saint John the Divine
1047 Amsterdam Avenue
New York, NY
212-662-2133
www.stjohndivine.org/Halloween.html
This gothic cathedral's Halloween
extravaganza includes a silent horror
movie with live organ music and a
closing procession of ghouls.

Washington Irving's Home

West Sunnyside Lane
Tarrytown, NY
914-591-1020
Listen to a reading of *The Legend
of Sleepy Hollow* at the author's
childhood home.

Bat Spectacular

Congress Avenue Bridge
Austin, TX
512-327-9721
Each night at dusk from March until
early November a colony of over one
million bats emerges from its home
under the bridge to forage for insects
across the way.

Monte Cristo

Route 92, Mountain Loop Highway
Granite Falls, WA
425-259-7911
Visit the abandoned mining town of
Monte Cristo.

Planning and making a costume continues to be the best way to get into the spirit of the holiday, especially if the supplies for it are scavenged or inexpensive or inventive. Saving bits and pieces for costumes and decorations can become a year-round project.

The next piece of equipment every child needs when venturing out to trick-or-treat is a Halloween goodie bag. Decorating a bag is a project a child can do on his or her own, or at a party where the totes are taken home as favors and used later on during the neighborhood rounds. Use the simple silhouette shapes that symbolize Halloween to turn a solid-color shopping bag into part of the costume. Cut the shapes out of black and orange construction paper and paste them on both sides of a good-sized paper shopping bag with sturdy handles. Each child can sign his or her name on the bottom corner for instant identification.

Dressed-up children are proud of their costumes, and one way to turn a helter-skelter run through the neighborhood into an enjoyable evening for everyone is to organize a Halloween parade, which adds pageantry to trick-or-treating. A neighborhood parade can include everyone who wants to participate—grown-ups, too! Plan a route through a local park, or arrange to block off some side streets to traffic. Hot apple cider served at the last stop will warm even the coldest bones.

A visit to a haunted house along the trick-or-treat route will make Halloween night memorable (or see pages 122-123 for some ideas on creating a haunted house of your own).

KID-PLEASING COSTUME IDEAS

This chapter contains step-by-step instructions for six irresistible costumes, from an impish devil and a sparkly fairy to a ferocious lion and Red Riding Hood. But if you are short on time or not skilled with a needle and thread, try these equally adorable non-sewing costume ideas.

FOREST SPRITE: Gather large fall leaves and glue gun, staple, or safety pin them all over a green or brown turtleneck and leggings (these can be old clothes, dyed). Attach more leaves to a headband. With face paint, make green circles around the eyes, a white mouth, and a brown face.

PIRATE: A striped pullover, a red vest, dark pants tucked into boots, and a bandana tied around the head are the basics. Add an eye patch made from black paper and tied on with elastic. Don't forget a large gold hoop earring and a cutlass, made of cardboard spray-painted silver.

BLACK CAT: The base clothes are a black turtleneck and tights. For a tail, stuff one leg from an old pair of black tights with rags and safety pin to the tights. Glue two small cardboard triangles to a headband, and add a black eye mask and face-paint whiskers.

FAIRY: For simpler instructions than the ones beginning on page 194, start with a plain, long-sleeved, white dress that is long and full. Make a cardboard crown and glue on glitter. Make a wand by gluing a cardboard star to the end of a stick. Fairy wings can be created by covering two hangers with tinfoil, bending the tops of the hangers sideways, and pinning them to the dress with large safety pins.

GOBLIN: Make a mask from a brown-paper bag that goes over the head and rests on the shoulders. Mark large eyes, a nose, and a mouth carefully and cut out. Trim the mask with glued-on crepe paper or construction paper (for wild hair) and draw on some scary goblin details with markers. An old bathrobe or dark sweatsuit is the only other thing needed.

ROBOT: For the head, spray-paint a paper bag silver and cut out eye holes. Attach pipe cleaners with duct tape for antennae, and draw square eyes, a nose, and a mouth with a marker. Cut a hole (for the head) in the bottom of a large cardboard box; cut out holes for the arms. Spray-paint silver or cover the box with aluminum foil. Glue on buttons, small paper cups, and other found objects to create the controls, or draw shapes for controls with a marker.

FORTUNE TELLER: Start with a full, long skirt and oversized white blouse. Wrap a necktie around the waist and a scarf around the head, and add a big hoop earring and lots of necklaces. A shawl and brightly colored lipstick, a pack of playing cards, and a crystal ball (a Styrofoam ball covered in foil) are the accessories.

SCARECROW: Cut holes for eyes and a nose out of a brown paper bag and draw a big mouth in a smile. Glue straw or strips of brown paper (or lots of tall dry weeds from a field) on top for hair. Put on a loose shirt and baggy pants and stuff straw or more strips into the sleeves and at the bottom of the pants, extending over the hands and shoes. Tie a cord around the wrists and ankles to keep the straw in. Top with a floppy hat that has straw or strips of paper glued inside so they hang down and stick out like scarecrow hair.

LADYBUG OR OTHER CRITTERS: Adapt this for other bugs, a turtle, or a bird. Cut two large pieces of oak tag or poster board in large circles and paint them red. Add small black dots. Cut an eyemask out of black construction paper, glue on pipe cleaners for feelers, and tie on with string. Create a sandwich board by stapling the two boards across the top, leaving an opening for the head. Wear black, green, or brown clothing appropriate to the critter.

- -

Carefree Trick-or-Treating

* **Accompany the kids** to costume parades and block parties.
* **Check that your child will not trip** on a costume that is too long or too big. Long hems can be sewn, or held in place with iron-on hem tape.
* Reflective tape and **glow-in-the-dark paints** can be used on costumes and trick-or-treat bags to make adults and kids more visible at night.
* **Beware of lit candles** and jack-o'-lanterns, burning leaves, and cigarettes, since most costume fabrics are not treated with flame retardants.

- -

MORE EASY COSTUME IDEAS AND INSPIRATIONS _ _ _ _ _ _ _ _ _ _

* Stimulate your creative imagination by scouring through mail-order catalogs, party circulars, and costume shops for ideas.

* Embellish any clothing—a solid-colored skirt, vest, leggings, sweatshirt, or cape—with bold cutout images sewn or painted on. Or cut fusible products, from the interfacing department at the local fabric store, into shapes and iron onto sweatshirts or other clothing. These products are also handy to give fabric weight (when you're making wigs or a skirt).

* If you have a few children, dress them in different animal costumes and have Dad dress as the zookeeper.

* Make a poncho to be worn over sweats or a leotard by cutting any large, fairly heavyweight piece of fabric, such as felt, satin, or brocade, into a donut shape. Embellish with cutouts.

* Instant mask: Pop the lenses from a pair of old sunglasses and decorate the rims with feathers, glitter, and rhinestones.

* Buy inexpensive bridal tulle to make a beautiful ballerina's skirt. A little girl can wear it over a leotard or shiny bathing suit. Hem then gather layers of fabric with an elastic band, which doesn't require much sewing.

* To keep warm on a cold Halloween night, pair a fleece sweatshirt with matching pants and add mouse ears or insect antennae on a headband.

* Use neon reflective tape, glitter, or brightly colored fabric paints to decorate clothing and create imaginative, eerie effects with a glow-in-the-dark look, which will also keep your child visible in the dark.

* Paint large brown paper bags with animal faces and cut two large holes for eyes. Use paint or markers to create whiskers, raccoon eyes, or a little dog nose.

FARMSTAND TRICK-OR-TREAT BOWL

MATERIALS

large flattish pumpkin, such as Rogue Vif d'Etampes (Cinderella)

foil or bowl that fits inside the pumpkin

vellum paper

floral u-pins

candy

TOOLS

carving knife

large spoon

Set out candy for trick-or-treaters or Halloween party guests in a pumpkin-shell container. A bed of hay, straw, or leaves in a big round platter completes the rustic look. A little sign suggesting portion control will draw attention to the candy supply, but it's unlikely anyone will heed the message.

1 Cut a wide opening in the top of the pumpkin. Scoop out the seeds and the pulp. Rinse the inside of the pumpkin with cool water and pat dry.

2 To keep the candy out of contact with the pumpkin flesh, line the interior of the pumpkin with foil or set a bowl inside the cavity.

3 Cut vellum paper in wide strips and roll it over lengthwise several times, crumpling it slightly to resemble a pie crust. Secure it to the cut rim of the pumpkin with floral u-pins (insert two pins at each point, overlapping them at different angles so they won't easily pull out). Adjust the "crust" and fill the lined pumpkin or the bowl with candy.

TRICK-OR-TREAT SURPRISES

MATERIALS

1 package cheesecloth

1 package orange cocktail-size paper napkins

1 package black cocktail-size paper napkins

orange and black jelly beans

black string licorice

plastic spiders

fake spiderwebbing (available from stores with Halloween supplies)

TOOLS

thumbtacks

Trick-or-treating has its origins in Irish traditions of long ago; these days kids often skip the trick but want their treat nonetheless. These little bundles are a fun way to wrap up candy for trick-or-treaters or party favors.

1 For about half the treats, cut 6-inch squares of double-layered cheesecloth. For the others, unfold an orange napkin. Unfold a black napkin and place it on top of the orange napkin at a 45-degree angle. Repeat with more napkins.

2 Pile handfuls of jelly beans in the center of each cheesecloth square and each set of napkins. Use the licorice string to tie each packet into a pouch and place a spider on each.

3 Place the bundles in a shallow bowl or tray. Set the platter on the spiderwebbing near the door. Pull the webbing around the platter at different angles, anchoring it to the table or a wall with thumbtacks.

SKELETON COSTUME

MATERIALS

1 yard white felt

face paint: 1 teaspoon cornstarch, ½ teaspoon cold cream, ½ teaspoon water

food coloring (optional)

TOOLS

pattern (see page 215) or life-size Halloween skeleton decoration (available in party supply stores)

fabric glue such as Sobo Premium Craft and fabric Glue

safety pins

small paintbrush

BASE GARMENTS

black sweatshirt

black sweatpants

black stretch one-size-fits-all gloves

On a dark Halloween night, whoever ventures out in this costume will scare everyone along the way! Let your trick-or-treater go rattling through the neighborhood—even the chilliest night won't bother this bag-o'-bones. Apply simple felt shapes to a black sweatsuit, and Mister or Miss Skeleton can stay outside in comfort.

1 Trace the skeleton bone pattern onto the white felt. Cut out.

2 Lay out the sweatshirt and pants and place the felt bones where appropriate. Measure the child so the elbow, shoulder, and knee joints are in the right places. Be sure the center the spine and ribcage. Secure the felt in place with safety pins.

3 Glue the felt bones down carefully with the fabric glue. Remove the pins. Cut the finger tips off the black gloves.

4 To make the face paint, mix the cornstarch, cold cream, and water. Add food coloring, if you like. If making more than one color, mix each color in its own muffin tin cup or film canister. Stir until well blended.

5 With the small paintbrush, paint the child's face with the face paint, being careful to avoid the area around the eyes.

Recycle It!

If you would like to wash and reuse this costume, sew the felt onto the sweats. You might find this easier to do if you open up the side seams of the sleeves and pants. After the felt has been sewn on, close up these seams.

FAIRY COSTUME

Make a little girl's dream come true with the fairy princess outfit. If made directly from the pattern, this costume is a size 2 or 3. If you need a larger size, simply follow the instructions to adjust the fit. It can be adjusted to a size 6 or 8.

patterns (see page 216)

MATERIALS

½ yard purple felt

1½ to 2 years lavender crinoline (108 inches wide)

2 to 2½ yards burgundy crinoline (108 inches wide)

lavender and burgundy thread

1 yard black ¾-inch-wide Velcro

8- by 8-inch scrap fuchsia felt

small artificial purple and pink flowers

green and silver glitter

½ yard green felt

¾ yard deep pink organza

½ yard ½-inch elastic

1⅓ yards 2-inch-wide wired green ribbon

TOOLS

patterns (see page 216)

hot glue gun and sticks

fabric glue, such as Sobo Premium Craft and Fabric Glue

pinking shears

BASE GARMENTS

burgundy or purple leotard and tights

SKIRT

1 For the waistband, measure the child around her waist. Add 8 inches. Cut a strip of purple felt that is 3½ inches wide by this measurement long. Fold in half lengthwise; press.

2 From the child's waist, measure the length you want for the skirt. Add 3 inches. Lay the lavender crinoline out on a flat surface and cut 2 pieces the width of the crinoline by the skirt length. Sew the crinoline lengths together to make one approximately 200-inch long strip. Repeat for the burgundy crinoline. Lay the burgundy crinoline strip on top of the lavender and sew together across the upper edge.

3 Using a double thickness of thread, sew ½-inch stitches right next to the stitching line across the entire top, pulling to gather as you go along. Pull this gathering to match exactly the purple felt strip length. Slip the gathered fabric into the purple felt waistband. Pin in place. Sew the bottom and the sides. Remove the pins.

4 Cut 3- or 4-inch scallops on the bottom of the lavender layer, all the way around. Repeat for the burgundy layer.

5 Sew two 3-inch strips of Velcro to the ends of the waistband, making sure that the hook (rough) side will face in and the loop (fuzzy) side will face out (this way the wings will not get caught on any exposed Velcro).

6 Using the leaf pattern, cut about 12 leaves from the fuchsia felt. Reserve 6 to 8 artificial flowers for the headdress. Pull the remaining flowers off their stems and hot glue one to each leaf. Let dry, and then shake off the excess. Pin the flowers on the skirt in a random pattern and hand sew in place. Remove the pins.

VEST

1 Adjust the vest patterns. Measure the child from the shoulder (at the neck) to the waist. Add 2 inches and adjust the front and back patterns vertically to this measurement on the adjustment lines if necessary. Measure around the child's chest, divide this number by 2, and adjust the back at the adjustment line to this measurement. Take the amount you increased the back, divide it in half, and add this amount to the front width at the adjustment line. Straighten out the shoulder lines. Don't adjust the neck or armholes until you cut out the pattern and sew it.

2 Use the adjusted pattern to cut out one back piece from the green felt. Cut out 4 front pieces: 2 green and 2 purple. Pin the green front pieces on top of the purple front pieces, making sure you have a left and a right side. Sew the back to the front at the shoulder seams, right sides together. Remove the pins and try on the child. Adjust where necessary along the shoulder seam (make neck hole a little larger? cut down width at arm?). See how the vest armholes will fit and mark where they should be cut a little larger if necessary. Remove the vest from the child and make the adjustments. Resew the shoulder seams if necessary. Pin and then sew the side seams. Remove the pins.

3 Place the vest on the child and mark with pins where the front overlaps. Remove from the child and attach the Velcro in the following way: On the child's right side of the vest, lift up the green pinned layer and pin a 4-inch strip of Velcro on the purple felt layer, facing inside. On the other front side, pin the opposite Velcro on the green layer, facing outside. Sew these in place. Hot glue the 2 layers of front felt together where necessary.

4 With the fabric glue, squeeze out decorative swirling designs on one outer side of the vest front. Sprinkle with the green glitter and let dry. Repeat for the other side and let dry. Turn the vest over and make little dots with the glue, keeping decorations $1/2$ inch away from the shoulder seam and top of neck. Sprinkle with glitter and let dry.

5 Attach Velcro to the vest: Cut a 2-inch strip of loop (fuzzy) Velcro and pin it at neck center back. Measure across the shoulders and cut 2 more strips loop (fuzzy) Velcro about 1/2 inch shorter than the shoulders are wide and attach one to the back of each shoulder, about 1/4 inch from the seam.

WINGS

1 Measure the child from the top of the spine at the neck to the wrist. Adjust the wing pattern so that the center back to the wrist is 2 inches longer than this measurement (for ease of movement). Make the pattern longer top to bottom, if desired.

2 Using this pattern and pinking shears, cut out a double layer of pink organza, aligning the fold with the fold mark on the pattern. Then cut out a double layer of burgundy crinoline, again aligning the folds. Sew the 2 pieces together across the top. Cut a purple felt strip, 1 inch wide by the length of the top, and pin it to the crinoline layer of the wing top. Sew together. Remove the pins.

3 Wrap the elastic around the child's wrist loosely enough to feel comfortable but not so loose as to fall off. Pin the ends where they meet and remove from the wrist. Sew as pinned and make a second one exactly the same. Attach one to each end of the felt strip at the top of the wings with a few stitches.

4 To attach the wings, take the 2-inch strip of hook (rough) Velcro that matches the Velcro at the vest center back and sew it onto the center of the felt strip on the wing. Put the vest on the child. Attach the Velcro loop strips that match the vest shoulders. Slip on the elastics at the wrists. At the child's shoulders, pin the wings to the vest. Remove the wings and vest, and pin the loop Velcro to the wings. Sew the Velcro in place. Remove the pins.

5 To decorate the wings, cut out 8 purple felt circles 1 1/2 inches in diameter. Make a fabric glue circle in the center of each and sprinkle on silver glitter. When dry, pin onto the crinoline layer of the wings. Have the child try on the wings. Correct the placement if necessary. Hand sew in place. Remove the pins.

HEADDRESS

1 Beginning in the center, sew the remaining artificial flowers onto the ribbon about 2½ inches apart. Gently place the ribbon around the child's head and twist to close it in a circle. Twist the dangling ends into ringlets that can droop down. Cut off ends if they are too long. Slip the headdress off the child.

2 Make little dots on the ribbon with fabric glue and sprinkle with silver glitter. Let dry.

DEVIL COSTUME

Who could be afraid of this imp of a devil? For an easier version, make just the tail and horns, then attach to red pants and a red headband. This makes about a size 4, but it can easily go larger; just make the cape longer.

CAPE

1 Adjust the cape pattern so that the length will come a bit below the child's hip. Using the adjusted pattern, cut out a double layer of felt, aligning the fold with the fold mark on the pattern. Try the cape on the child and see if you need to make any adjustments to the neck hole. The cape should overlap at the front by 1½ inches. If you make any adjustments to the neck, remember to extend the collar horizontally by the same amount before cutting it out.

2 Using the collar pattern, cut out 2 pieces of felt. Pin and sew the collar together along the sides and top (longer) edge, using a ¼-inch seam allowance. Turn right side out and top stitch ¼ inch from the edge around the sewn edge. Lay the unsewn bottom of the collar along the top edge of the cape, matching the center of the collar to the center back of the cape, and making sure the collar ends are equidistant to the front opening on both sides. Pin and sew the collar to the cape. Remove the pins and press the seam, including the edges of the cape next to the collar, in along the wrong side of the cape. If you like, topstitch ¼ inch from the edge along the sewn edge. Trim the seams.

3 Have the child put on the cape and mark where to place the Velcro coins at the top of the cape's placket. Sew 2 loop (fuzzy) coins to the child's right side of the cape, facing out. Sew the hook (rough) Velcro to the left cape placket, facing in.

HOOD

1 Using the hood pattern, cut out 4 pieces of felt. On each one, sew the dart seam closed (see the pattern), using a ¼-inch

MATERIALS

2 yards red felt

red thread

6 red ¾-inch Velcro coins

6 inches red ¾-inch-wide Velcro

about 6 ounces polyester fiberfill

TOOLS

patterns (see page 217)

BASE GARMENTS

red pants

red long-sleeve shirt

ghoulish costumes & clever disguises   **199**

seam allowance. With the right sides together, pin and then sew 2 pieces of felt from the back of the neck to the forehead, matching up the darts. Repeat for the lining, but leave a 3-inch opening in the back of the head seam to turn the whole hood right side out. Remove the pins.

2 With the right sides together, pin the lining to the outside at the neck/back seam and at the forehead front seam. Pin all areas in between. Sew the lining to the hood, all the way around, using a $1/4$-inch seam allowance. Remove the pins.

3 Turn the hood right side out by pulling through the hole. Hand stitch the hole closed. Topstitch $1/4$ inch all around the face opening, or iron it.

4 Sew 4 Velcro loop (fuzzy) coins in a square on the outside of the child's right flap. Sew two 3-inch strips of hook (rough) Velcro to the inside left flap.

5 Using the horn pattern, cut out 4 pieces of felt. Pin and then sew the pairs together, using $1/4$-inch seam allowances, leaving the base open. Remove the pins. Turn the horns right side out. Stuff with fiberfill. Pin the horns to the hood by matching their side seams to the dart seams and placing them equidistant from the center hood seam, about 2 inches down to either side. Hand sew securely in place. Remove the pins.

TAIL

1 Using the tail pattern, cut out 2 pieces of felt. Pin and then sew them together, using a $1/2$-inch seam allowance and leaving the upper end open and a hole in the side as marked on the pattern. Remove the pins. Turn the tail right side out. Stuff with fiberfill, using both openings. Hand stitch the side opening closed.

2 Pin the tail to the child's pants, about $1/2$ inch down from the waistband in the center of the back. Hand sew securely in place. Remove the pins.

LION COSTUME

The hooded sweatshirt and sweatpants of this easy-to-make costume will keep a child warm, making this a good choice for a cold October evening.

MATERIALS

¹/₃ yard tan felt

tan and yellow thread

about 6 ounces polyester fiberfill

¹/₃ yard fuzzy light tan felt

¹/₃ yard yellow felt

¹/₃ yard gold felt

2 yards transparent fishing line (optional)

1 foot ¹/₄-inch elastic (optional)

TOOLS

patterns (see page 218)

hot glue gun and sticks

BASE GARMENTS

yellow sweatpants

yellow hooded zip-up sweatshirt

tan one-size-fits-all gloves

1 Using the tail pattern, cut out 2 pieces of tan felt. Pin the 2 pieces together, then sew, using a ¹/₂-inch seam allowance and being sure to leave holes open as marked on pattern. Remove the pins.

2 Stuff the tail with fiberfill, using both holes. Hand sew the side hole closed. Pin the tail to the back of the pants, ¹/₂ inch below the waistband. Hand sew in place. Remove the pins.

3 Using the tail tip pattern, cut 2 pieces of the fuzzy light tan felt. Pin one piece around the tail, 4 inches up from the bottom end. Pin the second piece overlapping the other so the tail is completely encircled. Hand sew in place. Remove the pins.

4 Using the tail tip fringe pattern, cut out 8 pieces of felt—2 tan, 2 fuzzy light tan, 2 yellow, and 2 gold. Using the tail tip strip pattern, cut out one piece of tan felt. Lay the strip down flat and place the fringe strips on it perpendicularly, lining them up along the strip. Pin and then sew in place. Remove the pins. Wrap the strip around the top of the lion tail tip with the fringe going toward the tail and hand sew in place. You may want to put a few tacking stitches into the tail tip itself.

5 Using all the felt colors, cut at least 100 strips, ¹/₂ inch wide by 12 to 15 inches long. Measure around the opening of the sweatshirt hood. Add 4 inches. Cut a strip of tan felt, 2 inches wide by this measurement long. Lay this hood strip down on a flat surface and lay the ¹/₂-inch strips across it, alternating the colors and having differing lengths on each side of the strip. Be sure that there is an even distribution of strips along the hood strip. Pin the strips in place and then sew to the hood strip, about ¹/₄ inch from one edge. Remove the pins.

6 Pin the center of the hood strip to the center front of the outside of the sweatshirt hood. Pin around each side and let the 2 inches at each end dangle down at the neck line. Sew the strip to the

hood, being careful to sew only the strip, not the fringe pieces.
Remove the pins.

7 Have the child put the sweatshirt on. Trim the strips at the top so
his face shows well enough and he can see, or tack any wayward
strips to the hood.

8 To make the talons, use the talon pattern to cut out 10 pieces of
fuzzy light tan felt and 10 of yellow felt. Hot glue a yellow one to
each finger of the gloves on the palm side, $1/2$ inch from the tip.
Turn the gloves over and repeat with tan on the outer side, then
glue the tan and yellow felt together where they touch.

9 If you like, sew or tie fishing line to the tail tip and tie on an
elastic loop for the child to wear around his wrist and manipulate
the tail like a puppet. Adjust the length of the fishing line as
necessary.

WITCH COSTUME

Look who just flew in—the patchwork witch! Make the creation of this costume a joint venture: Witches-to-be will take great pride in deciding where the patches will go, and then helping to sew them on. Don't mind if little fingers make big stitches, the ragtag look is in style these days. And don't forget the broom—there's no better way to fly around the neighborhood. This makes a very loose, roomy size 6.

MATERIALS

2½ yards black stretch knit fabric

scrap black and white print fabric

scraps blue and red felt

¾ yard black felt

18- by 18-inch piece flat corrugated cardboard

TOOLS

patterns (see page 219)

pinking shears

compass

X-Acto knife

fabric and paper spray adhesive, such as S704 fabric and Foam Adhesive from BFG Goodrich

4-inch-diameter shipping tube

royal blue and red fabric markers

BASE GARMENTS

white tights

black turtleneck sweater

DRESS

1 Using the patterns cut out 2 body pieces and 2 sleeve pieces from the black knit. For the front of the dress, cut the neck opening of one body piece 1½ inches deeper, keeping it the same width at the shoulders (see pattern).

2 Pin the dress front and back together at shoulder seams, right sides together. Sew together using a ½-inch seam allowance. Remove the pins. Open up, right side facing up, and pin the sleeves in place, right sides together, matching the shoulder seam to the shoulder notch. Sew the armhole seam. Fold the garment, right sides together, along the shoulder seams. Pin the side seams together, including the sleeve seam, and sew closed. Remove the pins. Turn right side out.

3 Cut triangles of varying sizes out of the dress bottom and sleeve ends, for a slightly ragged look. Pin some of the triangles together, overlapping each triangle about ½ inch onto the next one, and create a strip that equals the circumference of the neck opening. Sew the triangles together and remove the pins. Pin this strip along the wrong side of the neck opening and sew it ¼ inch from the neck edge. Turn it right side out and top stitch it down ¼ inch from the edge.

4 For the patches, cut squares and rectangles from the scrap pieces, using the pinking shears and regular scissors. Put a few aside to add to the hat. Place the remaining patches randomly on the dress, pin in place, and sew down. Cut out one triangle piece from the felt and sew it onto the collar. Remove the pins.

HAT AND TIGHTS

1 Using the cone pattern, cut one piece of black felt. Pin the 2 straight edges to each other, and sew together using a $1/2$-inch seam allowance. Remove the pins. Clip off excess at top and turn right side out. Place on child's head and mark where the cone fits. Cut $1/4$ inch below this line.

2 Cut out 2 layers of black felt using the brim pattern. Center the cone on top of the brim pattern. Carefully mark the cone circle on the pattern. Remove the cone. Cut out the inner circle from the pattern. Place the pattern on the corrugated cardboard and trace the outer and inner circles. With the compass, draw another circle 1 inch smaller than the outer circle. With the X-Acto knife, cut the cardboard there. Draw a circle $1/2$ inch bigger than the inner circle. Cut there.

3 Spray adhesive on one side of the corrugated cardboard and one circle of the felt. Carefully center the corrugated cardboard on the felt. Repeat with the other side of the cardboard and the other piece of felt. Lay the brim pattern on the brim and trace the inner hole. Cut pie slices into the felt from the center out to this traced line. Place the cone on the brim, with the pie slices on the inside of the cone. Pin in a few places and try on the child. If the hat needs to be larger, make the pie slice cuts a little deeper and slightly stretch the cone felt if necessary. If it needs to be smaller, you can fix that later.

4 Now unpin, and spray adhesive onto the pie slices to glue inside the hat (use the brim pattern paper to cover the parts of the hat you don't want sprayed). Also spray the bottom 2 inches of the cone. When tacky, attach the glued pieces.

5 Cut a 2- by 26-inch strip of black felt and wrap it around the base of the cone to form a hat band, overlapping the excess. Sew or glue in place. If the hat was too big, layer strips of felt around the inner circumference of the hat opening to make it smaller. Glue or sew in place.

6 Sew a few patches randomly on the hat. Trim the outer brim with pinking shears.

7 Insert the shipping tube into one leg of the tights. Use the blue marker to make horizontal strips by drawing parallel circles, about ³/₄ inch apart, around the leg. Let dry. Repeat with the other leg, using the red marker.

RED RIDING HOOD COSTUME

Inspired by the favorite Grimm's fairy tale, this costume will turn any little girl into a dutiful granddaughter carrying provisions through the forest. Just add a wolf and the picture is complete. This costume is a size 6 or 8. You can make all or parts of it—the cape would work well in any color or pattern (say, in black for Zorro, or blue for a superhero).

MATERIALS

2½ yards red felt
(60 inches wide)

red and white thread

4 red ¾-inch Velcro coins

1 yard white felt

1 yard ¾-inch-wide white
Velcro

red acrylic or fabric paint

blue fabric marker

TOOLS

patterns (see page 220)

stencil brush

paring knife

potato

BASE GARMENTS

blue cotton knit dress

red tights

HOODED CAPE

1 Measure from the child's shoulder to the knee and adjust the cape pattern so that its full length comes to several inches below the knee. Using this pattern, cut out a double layer of red felt, aligning the fold with the fold mark on the pattern. Using the hood pattern, cut out 2 pieces of red felt. Using the hood facing pattern, cut out 2 pieces of red felt.

2 Pin and sew the back and top seams of the hood together, using a ½-inch seam allowance. Pin and sew the top of the facing pieces together, using a ½-inch seam allowance. Remove the pins. Iron open the seams.

3 Match the front of the facing to the front of the hood and pin in place, making sure the seams match up and the right sides are together. Sew a ¼-inch seam. Remove the pins. Press the seam open. Fold the facing in along this seam and pin to the inside of the hood. Sew the facing in place. Remove the pins. Turn the hood right side out again. Turn the facing/hood front edge back to the notch on the hood at the neck. Pin in place.

4 Pin the hood to the cape, right sides together, matching up the hood back seam with the cape center back notch. Make sure the hood opening is equidistant on both sides of the front cape opening. Sew the hood to the cape, using a ½-inch seam allowance, and securing the folded-back facing/hood edge. Stitch down the seam allowance to the cape neck.

5 Fold in both sides of the cape front ½ inch and sew down.

6 On the child's right side of the cape, on the inside along the folded-in edge, pin and sew a line of 4 hook (rough) Velcro coins, starting at the top and evenly spaced about every 2 inches. Pin and sew the loop (fuzzy) Velcro to the outside of the left side.

APRON

1 For the waistband, measure the child around her waist. Add 8 inches. Cut a strip from the white felt that is 3½ inches wide by this measurement long.

2 Using the bib pattern, cut out one piece of white felt. Sew the straps to the bib front at the shoulder seams, using a ½-inch seam allowance. Sew down the seam allowance.

3 Using the apron skirt pattern, cut out one piece of white felt. Make a small notch at the center front top.

4 Hand sew 2 parallel lines of stitches ½ inch apart along the top of the apron skirt. Gather the top of the apron skirt until it is about 4 inches wider than the bottom of the bib front. Pin the center top of the apron skirt to the center bottom of the white felt waistband. Matching edges, pin in place and sew together, using a ½-inch seam allowance. Pin the bottom of the bib to the apron/waistband seam, wrong sides facing, matching at center front. Sew in place. Bring the bib front up so it looks like an apron. Pin the waistband in place on top of the bib front and sew it down. Sew the excess seam allowance for the apron skirt up against the waistband on the inside.

5 To attach the white Velcro, cut 2 hook (rough) strips 6 inches long and attach to the inside of the back straps where they will meet up with the waistband. Cut 2 loop (fuzzy) strips 8 inches long and pin to the outside of one end of the waistband, one above the other horizontally. Sew in place. Cut 2 hook (rough) strips 8 inches long and attach on the other side of the fabric, to the wrong side of the waistband, sewing on the same stitching lines. Cut 2 loop (fuzzy) strips 8 inches long and attach these, one above the other, on the outside of the other waistband.

PAINTING THE DRESS AND APRON _

1 Using the stencil brush, paint red polka dots onto the dress skirt.

2 Using the blue fabric marker, draw vertical blue stripes, about 2 inches apart, on the bib front, back straps, and apron skirt.

3 Using the paring knife, cut the potato in half and then draw a flower, 1 to 1½ inches wide, on one of the halves. Cut away the excess potato around the flower shape. Apply red paint to it and stamp flowers in between the blue lines. This will be a little tricky where the apron is gathered to the waistband, but it is possible to smooth it out long enough to print. With the fabric marker, put blue dots in the middle of each flower.

resources

templates

spook-tacular paper garlands

See page 71 for instructions. Enlarge 200%.

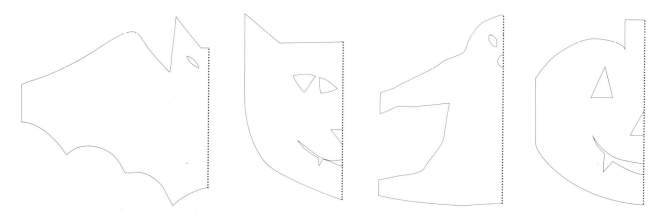

spooky felt pillows

See page 78 for instructions. Enlarge 425%.

skeleton costume

See page 193 for instructions.
Enlarge 800%.
One square = One inch

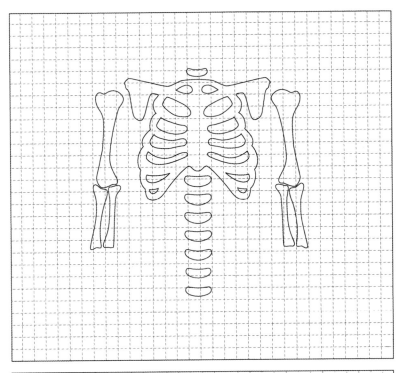

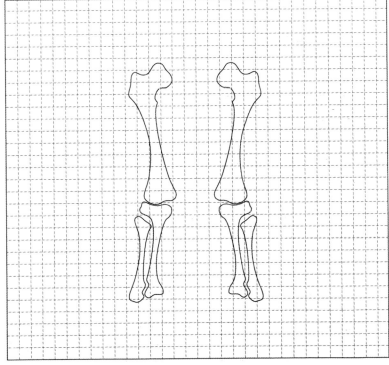

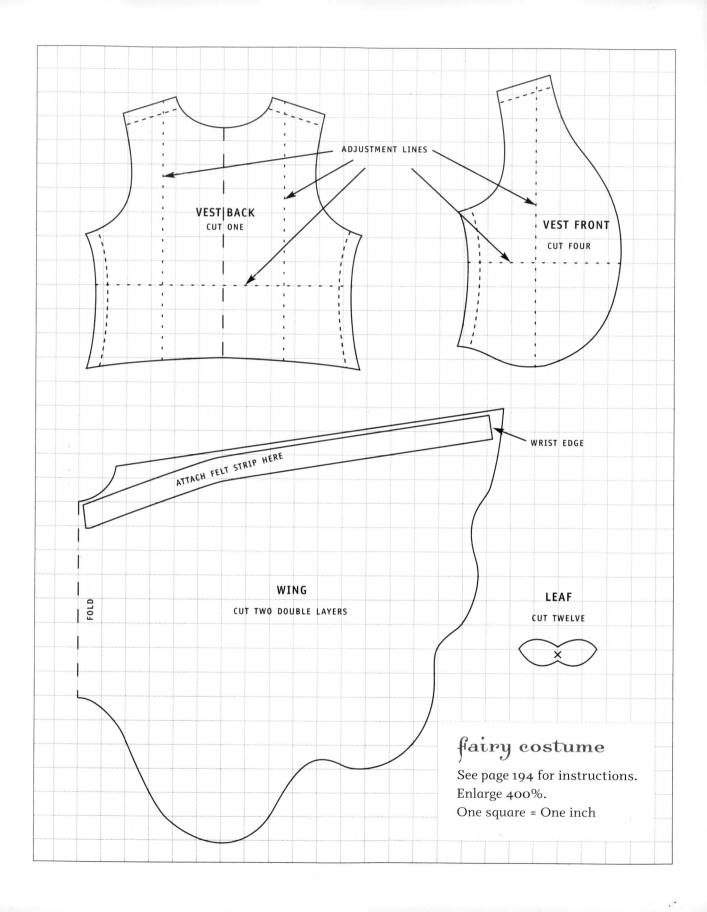

ADJUSTMENT LINES

VEST BACK
CUT ONE

VEST FRONT
CUT FOUR

ATTACH FELT STRIP HERE

WRIST EDGE

FOLD

WING
CUT TWO DOUBLE LAYERS

LEAF
CUT TWELVE

fairy costume

See page 194 for instructions.
Enlarge 400%.
One square = One inch

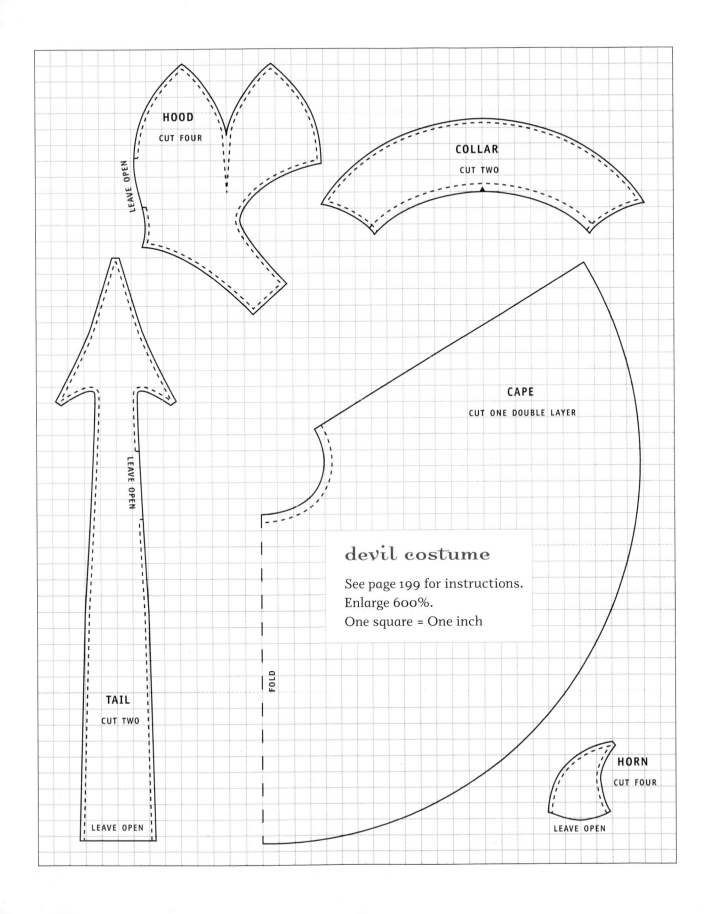

HOOD
CUT FOUR

LEAVE OPEN

COLLAR
CUT TWO

CAPE

CUT ONE DOUBLE LAYER

LEAVE OPEN

devil costume

See page 199 for instructions.
Enlarge 600%.
One square = One inch

TAIL

CUT TWO

FOLD

LEAVE OPEN

HORN
CUT FOUR

LEAVE OPEN

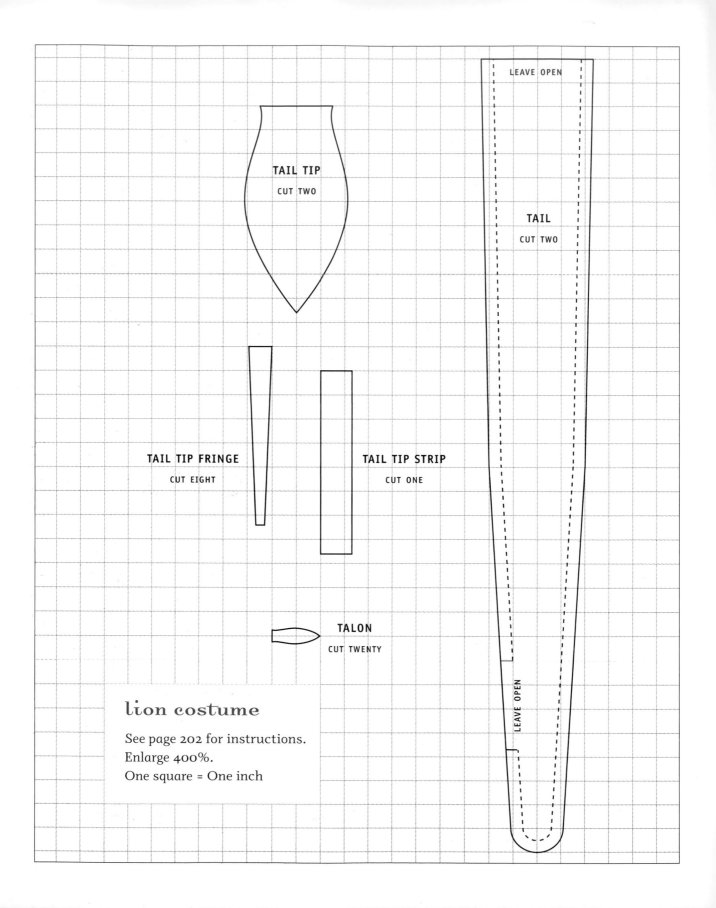

TAIL TIP

CUT TWO

TAIL

CUT TWO

LEAVE OPEN

TAIL TIP FRINGE

CUT EIGHT

TAIL TIP STRIP

CUT ONE

TALON

CUT TWENTY

LEAVE OPEN

lion costume

See page 202 for instructions.
Enlarge 400%.
One square = One inch

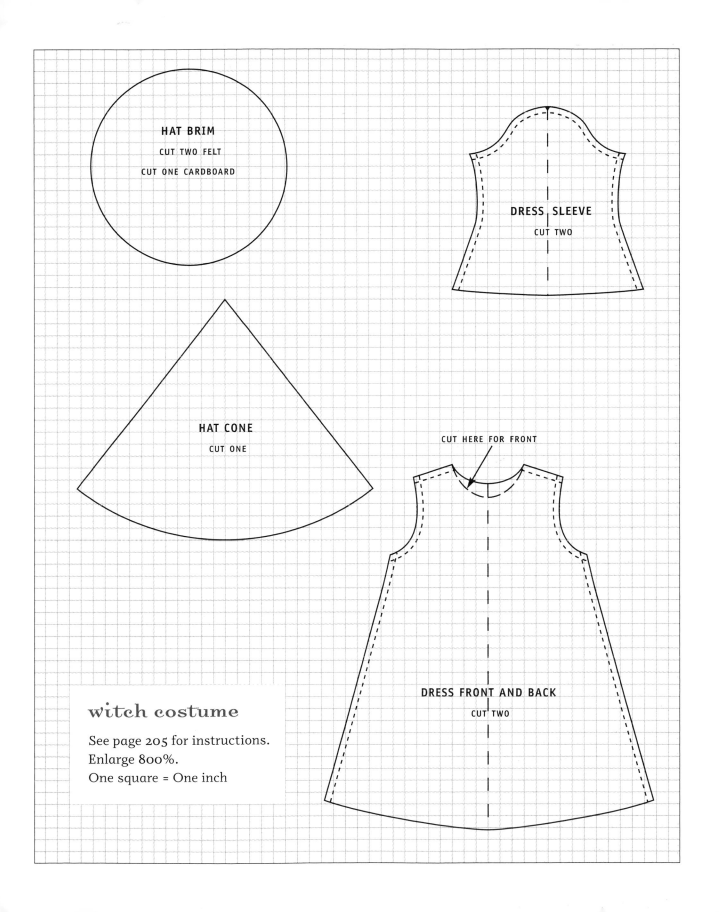

HAT BRIM
CUT TWO FELT
CUT ONE CARDBOARD

DRESS SLEEVE
CUT TWO

HAT CONE
CUT ONE

CUT HERE FOR FRONT

DRESS FRONT AND BACK
CUT TWO

witch costume

See page 205 for instructions.
Enlarge 800%.
One square = One inch

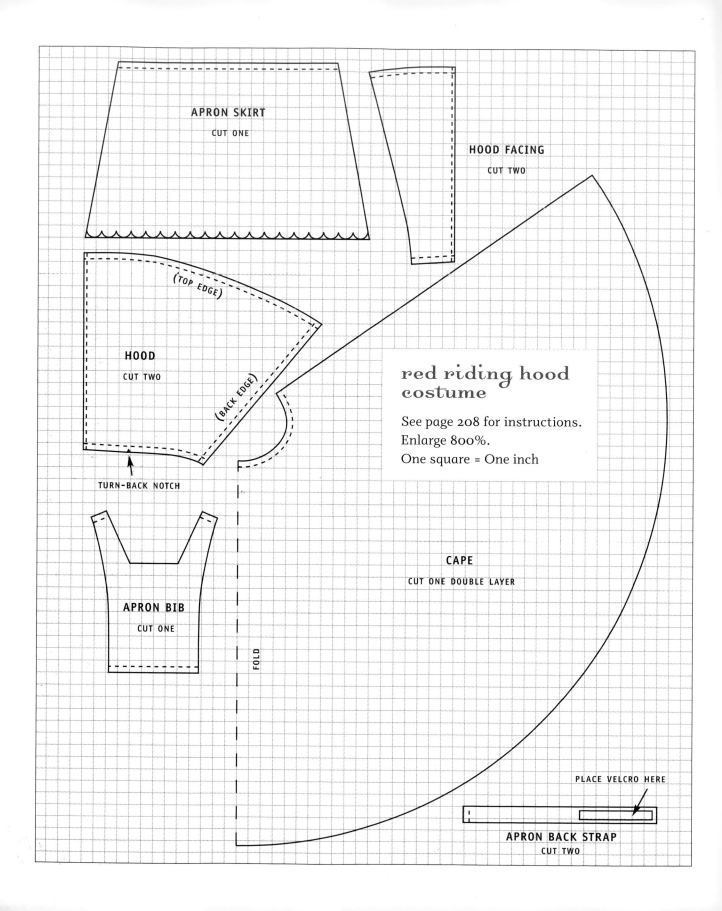

APRON SKIRT

CUT ONE

HOOD FACING

CUT TWO

(TOP EDGE)

HOOD

CUT TWO

(BACK EDGE)

TURN-BACK NOTCH

red riding hood costume

See page 208 for instructions.

Enlarge 800%.

One square = One inch

APRON BIB

CUT ONE

FOLD

CAPE

CUT ONE DOUBLE LAYER

PLACE VELCRO HERE

APRON BACK STRAP

CUT TWO

metric equivalent charts

The recipes in this book use the standard United States method for measuring liquid and dry or solid ingredients (teaspoons, tablespoons, and cups). The information on this chart is provided to help cooks outside the U.S. successfully use these recipes. All equivalents are approximate.

METRIC EQUIVALENTS FOR DIFFERENT TYPES OF INGREDIENTS

A standard cup measure of a dry or solid ingredient will vary in weight depending on the type of ingredient. A standard cup of liquid is the same volume for any type of liquid. Use the following chart when converting standard cup measures to grams (weight) or milliliters (volume).

Standard Cup	Fine Powder (e.g., flour)	Grain (e.g., rice)	Granular (e.g., sugar)	Liquid Solids (e.g., butter)	Liquid (e.g., milk)
1	140 g	150 g	190 g	200 g	240 ml
3/4	105 g	113 g	143 g	150 g	180 ml
2/3	93 g	100 g	125 g	133 g	160 ml
1/2	70 g	75 g	95 g	100 g	120 ml
1/3	47 g	50 g	63 g	67 g	80 ml
1/4	35 g	38 g	48 g	50 g	60 ml
1/8	18 g	19 g	24 g	25 g	30 ml

USEFUL EQUIVALENTS FOR COOKING/OVEN TEMPERATURES

	Farenheit	Celcius	Gas Mark
Freeze Water	32° F	0° C	
Room Temperature	68° F	20° C	
Boil Water	212° F	100° C	
Bake	325° F	160° C	3
	350° F	180° C	4
	375° F	190° C	5
	400° F	200° C	6
	425° F	220° C	7
	450° F	23° C	8
Broil			Grill

USEFUL EQUIVALENTS FOR LIQUID INGREDIENTS BY VOLUME

1/4 tsp	=					1 ml
1/2 tsp	=					2 ml
1 tsp	=					5 ml
3 tsp	=	1 tblsp	=	1/2 fl oz	=	15 ml
2 tblsp	=	1/8 cup	=	1 fl oz	=	30 ml
4 tblsp	=	1/4 cup	=	2 fl oz	=	60 ml
5 1/3 tblsp	=	1/3 cup	=	3 fl oz	=	80 ml
8 tblsp	=	1/2 cup	=	4 fl oz	=	120 ml
10 2/3 tblsp	=	2/3 cup	=	5 fl oz	=	160 ml
12 tblsp	=	3/4 cup	=	6 fl oz	=	180 ml
16 tblsp	=	1 cup	=	8 fl oz	=	240 ml
1 pt	=	2 cups	=	16 fl oz	=	480 ml
1 qt	=	4 cups	=	32 fl oz	=	960 ml
				33 fl oz	=	1000 ml

USEFUL EQUIVALENTS FOR DRY INGREDIENTS BY WEIGHT

(To convert ounces to grams, multiply the number of ounces by 30.)

1 oz	=	1/16 lb	=	30 g
4 oz	=	1/4 lb	=	120 g
8 oz	=	1/2 lb	=	240 g
12 oz	=	3/4 lb	=	360 g
16 oz	=	1 lb	=	480 g

USEFUL EQUIVALENTS FOR LENGTH

(To convert inches to centimeters, multiply the number of inches by 2.5.)

1 in	=			2.5 cm
6 in	=	1/2 ft	=	15 cm
12 in	=	1 ft	=	30 cm
36 in	=	3 ft	= 1 yd =	90 cm
40 in	=			100 cm = 1 m

photography credits

Numbers refer to page numbers.

Matthew Bensen: 61

Ryan Benyi: 118 (right), 137

Kinda Clineff: 86-87

Susie Cushner: 102 (center), 118 (center), 125, 127, 128, 144 (center), 149

Roy Gumpel: 10, 13

Michael Luppino: 144 (left), 145

Andrew McCaul: 5, 8, 12 (bottom & center), 14, 16, 17, 18, 19, 24, 27, 28, 31, 33, 34, 36, 39, 41, 45, 46, 48, 51, 53, 55, 56, 58 (center), 62, 66, 82, 84, 89, 90, 92, 93, 143, 146, 147, 150, 174, 179, 189

Debra McClinton: 118 (left), 175, 178

Keith Scott Morton: 6, 12 (top), 21, 22, 58 (top & bottom), 65, 69, 70, 73, 74, 77, 79, 81, 95, 96, 99, 116, 122, 123, 180, 182 (top & center), 184, 185, 187, 190, 192, 195, 198, 200, 203, 204, 207, 209, 211, 212

Marcus Nilsson: 100, 102 (top), 119, 169, 171 (2nd from top, 3rd from top, bottom)

Steven Randazzo: 2, 42 (all), 43, 117, 121

Charles Schiller: 102 (bottom), 107, 111, 144 (right), 155, 158, 160, 163, 164, 165, 166, 171 (top), 172, 176, 177, 182 (bottom)

Evan Sklar: 130, 132, 133, 139, 177

index